This Annual belongs to:

D0188361

....

....

A very special life!

illustrated by Clive Powell

*The story of Olave,
Lady Baden-Powell,
the World Chief Guide*

February 22nd is Thinking Day, when we think about Brownies and Guides all over the world. But do you know why February 22nd was chosen? The main reason was because it was the birthday of our Founder, Lord Baden-Powell and, by coincidence, the birthday of the most special Guide of all – the World Chief Guide, Olave, Lady Baden-Powell, who was born 100 years ago in 1889.

◄ **1** Olave St Clair Soames was born at Stubbing Court, near Chesterfield in Derbyshire. As a girl she loved animals and had many pets, including doves, ponies, and a spaniel called Doogy. She lived happily although her family moved house a lot and by the time she was ten years old she had lived in six houses!

▲
2 When Olave grew up she wanted to do something useful with her life. She applied to become a nurse in London but was turned down because she was too young.

◄ **3** In 1912, when Olave was twenty-two years old, she and her father went on a cruise to the West Indies. As they waited to board the ship they saw a little group of Scouts being inspected by their Founder, Lieutenant-General Sir Robert Baden-Powell. 'B-P' was also to be a passenger on the *SS Arcadian*.

4

4 B-P and Olave found they had ▶ a lot in common – including birthdays, although B-P was quite a lot older than Olave. He had seen her out walking her dog in London two years before and remembered her by the way she walked! By the end of the year they were married.

5 Olave threw herself into helping her husband with Scouting. She went with him to many camps and rallies and soon became almost as popular as B-P himself!

▲
6 In 1916 Olave started to help the growing Girl Guide organisation and became County Commissioner for Sussex. She travelled around the county helping to set up new Guide units.

7 Olave and B-P bought a ▶ house in the countryside and called it 'Pax Hill', because 'Pax' means 'peace'. Here their three children grew up and many Guides and Scouts came to camp in the gardens as well!

◀ 8 They travelled to many countries together visiting Guides and Scouts, who came long distances just to see them. One night they had to lean out of their train window dressed only in coats and hats over their night clothes to shake hands with Indian Scouts!

9 Guiding quickly spread ▶ around the world and in 1924 the first World Camp was held at Foxlease in Hampshire. It had been Olave's idea to bring Guides and Girl Scouts from all over the world together and the camp was very successful. In 1930 she was made World Chief Guide.

10 B-P was getting older and he and Olave went to live in Kenya, where the weather would be better for his health. In 1941 he ▼

died, aged eighty-three, and for a while Olave was lost without him. She came back to England, where it was wartime.

11 When the war finished she travelled around Europe helping Guides and Scouts to get started again in countries where Guiding and Scouting had been forbidden during the war.

12 For another 25 years she visited Guides and Scouts all over the world, travelling hundreds of thousands of miles.

13 In 1967 she toured Australia and the Guides liked her so much that they said they would each like to buy her an ice-cream as a 'thank you' for coming to visit them. As that would make more ice-cream than she could possibly eat, they decided to put the money into a special fund to help Guides in poorer countries—and so the 'Ice-Cream Fund' was born.

14 In 1970, she retired from travelling to live at Hampton Court. She kept in touch with the worldwide family of Guides and Scouts by writing letters and articles – and every Thinking Day they kept in touch with her as she was overwhelmed with cards and greetings.

15 Lady Baden-Powell died, aged eighty-eight, in June 1977 and her ashes were buried in B-P's grave at Nyeri in Kenya. In Westminster Abbey there is a memorial to remind us of them both. On the nearest Saturday to Thinking Day every year, Brownies, Guides, Cubs and Scouts lay flowers on it to say a big 'thank you' .

Gift Cards

written by Jane Wilson   illustrated by Kim Collins

There are lots of lovely greetings cards in the shops these days. Some of the nicest ones have little presents on them. The trouble is that these are usually expensive, costing perhaps two or three weeks' pocket money. If you make your own cards, you can not only save money, but you can give your friends and relations something much more special as well. Here are three ideas for gift cards to make yourself.

The wise old owl

This owl mobile makes a lovely card to send to a Brownie friend on Thinking Day, or perhaps you would like to make it for Brown Owl to say 'thank you' for all the hard work she does so that you can enjoy Brownie meetings.

You will need:

tracing paper
a soft pencil
a piece of stiff brown paper 13.5cm x 15cm
scissors
4 white round sticky labels 1.5cm across
sewing thread
sticky tape
glue
a piece of stiff yellow paper
15cm x 21cm (A5 size)
an envelope 11.5cm x 16.5cm (C6 size)

1. Trace the owl shape shown here. Turn the tracing paper over and put it pencil side down on the brown paper. Now very carefully draw over the lines again so that you leave the owl shape marked on the brown paper. Move the tracing paper along and repeat. You now have two owls drawn on the brown paper.

2. Cut out both owl shapes. To cut out the hole for the face, make a small hole in the middle and then make cuts from this towards the lines. You now have room to get your scissors in to cut round the lines.

3. Cut two short pieces of sewing thread and stick the end of each one onto a sticky label. Put another sticky label on top of each so that the thread is trapped in the middle.

4. Lay one owl shape on the table and position the sticky labels in the face hole for its eyes. Using very small pieces of sticky tape, carefully stick the thread to the card so that the eyes will hang in the right place.

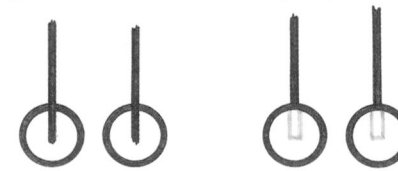

5 Cut another piece of thread about 50cm long and use sticky tape to stick it in the middle of the owl's head.

6 Carefully glue the second owl shape over the top of the first one to cover up all the sticky tape.

7 From the spare brown paper cut two squares about 3cm x 3cm. In one of these make a cut from one edge to the middle. Put the end of the long thread through the cut and stick it to the card with sticky tape. Glue the other square of paper over the top. Wind the thread around the square.

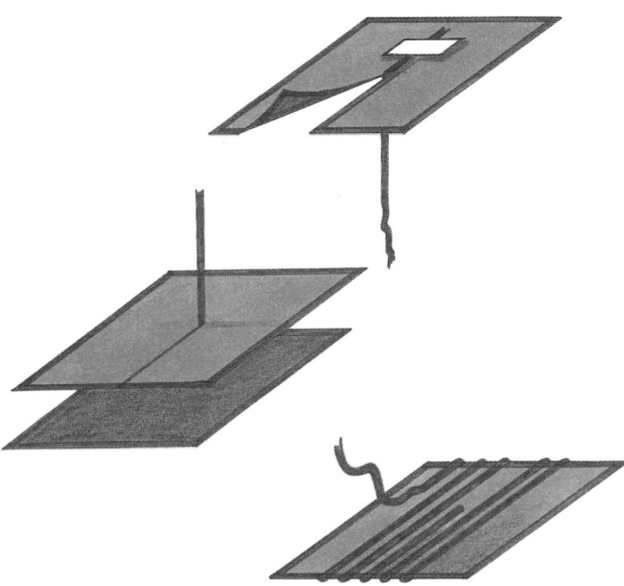

8 Fold the yellow paper carefully in half. Make a cut about 1cm long in the middle of the top edge on the front of the card. Put the thread through this so that the owl hangs in the middle of the card and the square with the thread wound round hangs on the inside.

9 Write a message in the card, put it in the envelope, and it's ready to send!

Stamp bookmark

A gift card for Father's Day, or for Dad's, a brother's or an uncle's birthday.

You will need:

6 to 12 used stamps (either bought from a stamp shop or soaked off old envelopes)
a piece of thin card approx 5cm by 16.5cm
glue
2 pieces of clear sticky-backed plastic slightly larger than the card
scissors
double-sided sticky tape
a piece of stiff paper 21cm x 21cm
an envelope 11cm x 22cm (DL size)

1 Arrange the stamps on the card. When you are pleased with the design, carefully glue them in place.

2 Stick one piece of sticky-backed plastic over the front of the bookmark and the other over the back. Trim the edges neatly.

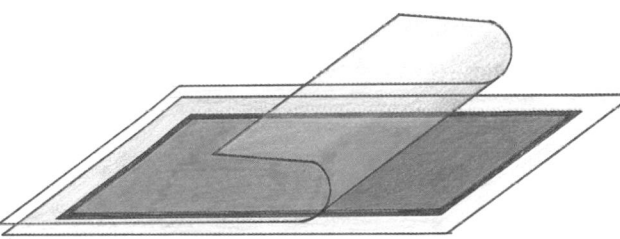

3 Fold the stiff paper carefully in half. Use two small pieces of double-sided sticky tape to stick the bookmark in the centre of the card.

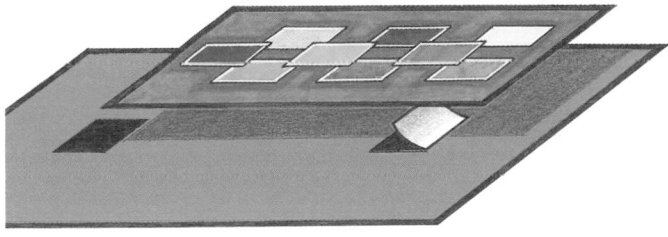

4 Write a message inside and put the card in the envelope.

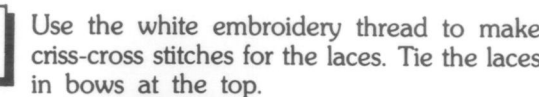

4 Use the white embroidery thread to make criss-cross stitches for the laces. Tie the laces in bows at the top.

5 Cut a piece of embroidery thread about 25cm long. Using the embroidery needle, thread one end through the back corner of each skate and tie in place. Fold the thread in half so that the two skates lie side by side and tie a knot about half way down to make a loop to hang over the tree.

Get your skates on

The present on this pretty Christmas card is a decoration to hang on the tree.

You will need:

tracing paper
a pencil
scissors
pins
12cm x 18cm red felt
red sewing thread
a fine needle
white embroidery thread
a large embroidery needle
2 paper clips 4cm long
a piece of stiff green paper
15cm x 21cm (A5 size)
an envelope 11.5cm x 16.5cm (C6 size)

6 Ask a grown-up to cut off the middle part of the paper clip with a pair of pliers. Carefully push the ends of the outside part between the stitching at the heel and toe of each skate to form the blade.

1 Trace the shape shown here and cut it out to make a pattern.

2 Using the pattern, cut the shape in felt four times. Pin the pieces together in twos to make two skates.

3 Using neat stitches, sew around each skate down the back, under the foot and around the toes. There is no need to sew where the laces go.

7 Fold the piece of green paper in half and make a cut about 1cm long in the middle of the top edge on the front. Put the embroidery thread through the cut so that the skates hang in the centre of the card and the knot is on the inside.

8 Write a message in the card and put it in the envelope.

A Day at Martin Mere

*written and photographed
by Michael Edwards*

On a bright but cold day in March, four Brownies from the 4th Fulwood Pack in Preston spent a day at the Wildfowl Trust's nature reserve at Martin Mere in Lancashire.

This wonderful sanctuary is situated on land which was once the largest lake in the country. The reserve is well known to birdwatchers as a favourite place for ducks, geese and swans to spend the winter in Britain.

Between October and March, thousands of people come to the reserve to watch the waterfowl from wooden 'hides'. Looking from these sheltered places visitors can see birds without disturbing them.

The most graceful birds to visit Martin Mere are the Whooper and Bewick swans. They fly in from Iceland and Siberia to spend their winters in the warmer south. Ten years ago these snow-white birds were rare in this area. Today in very cold weather there may be 300 or more here.

If that sounds like a lot of birds, it isn't really. Not compared to the numbers of Pink-footed geese which also fly down from the north. There may be up to an amazing 15,000 of these! They have a loud honking call. We first saw some of them in the air, flying in a 'V' shape against a cold blue sky. The geese settled in a field near one of the hides, where we could see them quite clearly through

The Brownies plot their route around Martin Mere on the big display board.

binoculars. They were eating the short grass which they graze like sheep.

As well as the wild birds, Martin Mere has a very large collection of tame ducks, geese and swans from all over the world. Some of them were very colourful indeed, as you can see from the photographs overleaf!

One of the most interesting is the Hawaiian goose. The Wildfowl Trust rescued it from extinction by breeding it in captivity. Without the work of the Wildfowl Trust, this gentle, friendly goose would no longer be with us.

As the photographs on this and the next two pages show, we had a super day at Martin Mere. So will you, if you visit the reserve!

The Brownie Annual would like to thank the staff of Martin Mere for their help in producing this feature.

We were quite surprised to see that the roof of the Martin Mere visitor centre was covered with grass. This makes the building blend into the countryside when seen by the birds as they fly over. Sometimes ducks even make their nests on the roof.

Gillian Taylor made friends with this lovely Hawaiian goose.

Sonia Westhead decides to take a closer look through binoculars while Emma Heald tried to take a photograph of the birds.

The Brownies look out across the reserve from the top level of the Manchester hide.

The view from the Manchester hide, with Greylag geese in the foreground and Whooper swans and ducks in the background.

◀ One of the most colourful ducks is the drake Carolina duck, or North American wood duck.

The Mandarin is a real dandy, too. In the wild, this duck lives in Eastern Asia and Japan. The drab-coloured female is seen behind the male.
▼

The Black Swan from Australia and Tasmania was truly magnificent.
▼

▲
We called this pond 'swan lake'. Dozens of Bewick and Whooper swans gather to feed in the shallow water.

·Puzzle out·
Norway

written by Jane Wilson
illustrated by Jill Gibbon

Hello!
I'm Inger - Lise   and I'm Guri . . . .
We're both Brownies in Norway. We have
different uniforms because there are two
different sorts of Brownies in our country.
Guri's Brownies are run by the YWCA and
are called Meise. They wear khaki dresses
and yellow scarves. Inger - Lise wears a
grey shirt and a blue skirt or trousers with a
tartan scarf. Her Brownies are part of the
Norwegian Guide and Scout Association
and are called Småspeidere which means
'little Guides'.

Try to find where we live in an atlas – Norway is in the north of Europe. It's a very long, thin country – over 1,800km long, but in the narrowest place only 6.3km wide! Much of the land is mountains, lakes and rocks. It is very beautiful, but it's not much good for farming and only three per cent of Norway is suitable for growing crops and keeping animals. Perhaps you'll be able to visit us one day, but until then you can find out more about Norway by doing these puzzles.

About a quarter of Norway is covered by forest and timber is an important industry. According to folklore there are creatures called trolls who live in the forests and mountains and all Norwegian Brownies know about two trolls called Karius and Baktus who will make holes in our teeth if we don't look after them. There are ten trolls hiding from the foresters in this picture – can you find them?

Because timber is so plentiful, most of the houses in Norway are built of wood. In the picture on the right you can see a traditional building made of whole logs. Modern houses are built from planks and although they might look odd to you, if you came inside you would find that they are very similar to your house. Our electricity is cheap because it is made from water power, so we are able to keep our houses warm and light through the long winter.

Like all Norwegians, we Brownies love to be outdoors. Most Norwegian families own a log cabin somewhere in the mountains or by a lake or fjord and spend as much time there as they can. In winter our favourite pastime is skiing, a sport which was invented in Norway. Children learn to ski at an early age so that the whole family can go out together at weekends to follow some of the many ski trails which are marked out in the countryside. These three Brownies are all following different trails, but only one of them will reach the log cabin – can you work out which one?

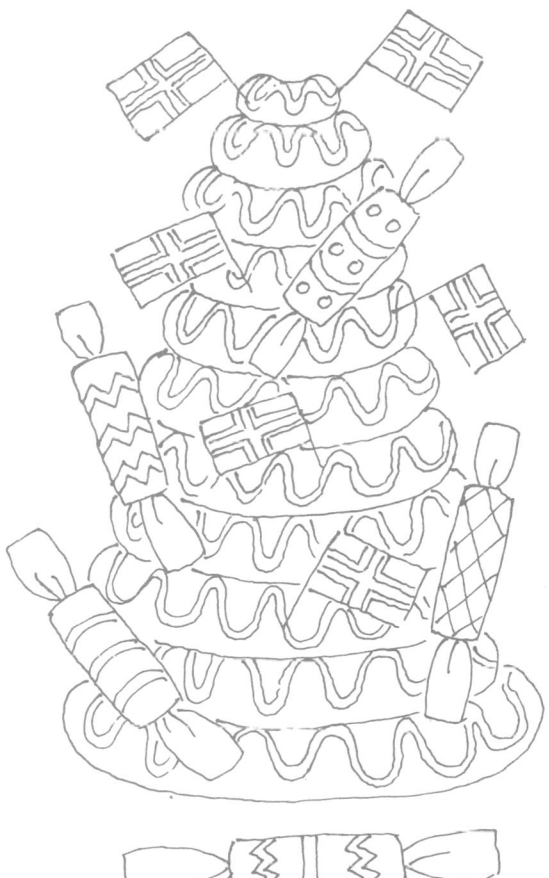

We have lots of good food in Norway, but things like vegetables and meat are quite expensive because of the small amount of land available for farming. It is usually easy to get good fish in Norway though, because nowhere is very far from the sea and there are lots of rivers where fish like salmon and trout are caught. One of our favourite things for breakfast is a brown cheese made from goat's milk. It looks a bit like caramel, and tastes quite sweet too. We cut it into thin slices with a special slicer and eat it on bread or crispbread.

On special occasions like weddings and confirmations we have a cake called a kransekake which means 'wreath cake'. Rings of different sizes are baked from almonds, sugar and egg whites and are piled on top of each other to make a tall tower. The picture on the left shows what a kransekake looks like, but you will have a much better idea if you colour it in. The cake rings are a lovely golden–brown colour and the dribbles of icing are usually white. It is decorated with our Norwegian flag, which is a blue cross with a white border on a red background, and with brightly–coloured crackers. When you've finished it should look good enough to eat!

15

A bouquet for Barbara

written by Ann Hillyer   illustrated by Mark Viney

"Now before you race out of the door, girls," reminded Brown Owl as the Pack Meeting drew to a close, "you won't forget what Tawny told you to bring next Tuesday, will you?"

"Fifty pence!" chorused the Brownies, all except one small, dark-haired girl who stood by the piano, hanging her head forlornly.

"That's right – fifty pence towards the cost of the outing," said Tawny. "I'm sure you're all looking forward to going to the Raindrop Theatre. Those of you who went last year will remember what fun it was. And you younger ones who haven't been before will have a marvellous time!"

Lesley Roberts grinned and nudged her newest friend, Paula Tate, who had recently moved into Birchborough and joined the Pack.

"The Raindrop Theatre's fantastic!" Lesley told Paula as they began to stroll down the lane. "It's specially built for young people's groups, and it's all pink and gold, with crystal chandeliers – like something out of a fairytale!"

Paula gave a shiver of excitement. "I've never been to a proper theatre before," she sighed.

"I'd like to go on the stage when I'm older," confided Lesley. "I'm doing tap and modern dancing now, as well as ballet. I'd like to go to speech and drama lessons, too, but they're so expensive."

"You'd make a good actress, Lesley," said Paula warmly. "You were super the other evening, when Brown Owl was getting us all to audition for the old folks' Christmas entertainment. I do hope I'm in it!"

"Oh, we'll all be in it," answered Lesley as they crossed the road and headed towards Paula's house. "At least, Brown Owl *likes* to give everyone a part, but I don't know how she's going to include Barbara!"

Barbara Barnes was also a newcomer to the Birchborough Pack. In fact, she had come along for the first time on the same day as Paula. However, the two eight-year-olds were as different as could be. Paula was bouncy and bubbly, with a merry grin and plenty to say.

By contrast, the small, dark Barbara had remained something of an outsider, despite the Leaders' attempts to draw her into the fun. She always seemed to be the last one chosen for a team game, and the first to slip away when meetings ended. Whenever she opened her mouth to say something, the words seemed to stick.

"It's a pity Barbara's got such a terrible stammer," remarked Paula, unlatching the gate. "I know she can't help it, but it does make conversation difficult. She's been here a month now, and I still don't know what hobbies she's got, or what she likes doing."

"Well, I don't much care," declared the forthright Lesley. "I'm not so sure I feel sorry for Babyish Babs – she probably mopes about and puts on that stammer just to get attention. I've heard of people doing that."

"Yes, but I don't think Barbara would, somehow," Paula said thoughtfully. "I know we're the same age, but she seems so much younger, and I can't help feeling sorry for her. I'd like to make friends."

"Well, don't forget you're sitting with me on the bus when we go to the theatre!" put in Lesley.

"I shan't," grinned Paula. "Anyway, I heard

others behind her. Once or twice Barbara ventured to start a conversation.

"The B-B-B-Brownie entertainment," she faltered, "d-d-do you think B-B-Brown Owl will want me to b-b-be in it, because . . ."

"I shouldn't think so," said Lesley shortly. "She's got plenty of us to choose from for the speaking and singing parts. You'll be able to hide at the back or in a corner, I expect, and do nothing – just like you do at Pack Meetings."

Barbara bit her lip, and tears welled up in her eyes. Lesley pretended not to notice.

"We're nearly there, girls!" called Tawny from the front of the bus. "Now, don't forget, learn as much as you can by watching the show, because next meeting Brown Owl and I will be giving out the parts for our entertainment. We're going to do a short sketch, some folk dances and finish up with some singing. Miss Paget, my sister who teaches music, is coming to play the guitar, and she has asked for some good singers!"

Lesley could not resist boasting to Barbara. "My cousin has singing lessons with Miss Paget," she told the younger Brownie with pride. "She's very particular about the pupils she takes. I might be going to her in September, if she thinks I'm good enough!"

"I-I like singing," began Barbara hesitantly, but the bus had stopped and Lesley was rushing out of her seat to make sure of joining her friends.

The theatre foyer was crowded as the pack were directed to their seats, three rows from the stage.

"Budge up, Stella," urged Lesley. "I want to sit next to Paula!"

"What about Barbara?" asked Jane, folding up her coat and sitting on it.

"Oh, she'll be all right at the end of the row," answered Lesley offhandedly. "I shouldn't think it will matter where she sits – she probably won't be the least bit interested!"

But once the huge velvet curtain rose, the whole audience was spellbound, including Barbara. The story unfolded about an African Prince who had quarrelled with his father, an expert huntsman. The son was forced to leave the kingdom and travel through the jungle, existing only by the help of the living creatures

Tawny telling Brown Owl that Barbara won't be coming on the outing. I didn't hear why."

But there was a surprise in store on the day of the outing, for Barbara was there with the others, waiting for the bus outside the hall.

"We're very glad Barbara could join us, after all," announced Brown Owl. "Unfortunately her father has been taken to hospital, and Mrs Barnes had to go with him. It's a good job there's plenty of room on the bus for a little one! And, Lesley – I'd like you to sit with Barbara, if you will."

"But I've promised to sit with Paula!" burst out Lesley at once. "And you know we should always keep our promises, Brown Owl."

"I know," Brown Owl went on, kindly but firmly, "but just for once I should like you to remember your Brownie Promise, Lesley – the bit about thinking of others and not ourselves."

"But what about Paula?" cried Lesley, as the bus rolled up.

"Paula has agreed to squeeze in with Jane and Stella at the back," said Brown Owl, "and if we don't all hurry up, we shall be late arriving at the theatre, and they may not let us in! Now, let's get moving, girls!"

The journey passed happily for everyone except Barbara and Lesley. The older girl sat glowering moodily out of the window. She felt irritated by the merry chatter of Paula and the

he loved. Some of the dancers were dressed as exotic birds, and others wore the masks of animals. The music was so beautiful that everyone listening was silent with admiration.

Just when the Prince had decided to stay and live with the animals, one of the birds brought him a message that his father was grieving for him. Back he journeyed to the beautiful palace, followed by all his new friends, and of course the story ended happily, with the King promising never to go hunting again.

As a tumult of clapping broke out, the Prince stepped forward and spoke to the audience.

"We are going to end with a song that I hope many of you will know," he said. "The words will be lowered on a screen for you to see. And perhaps two of you would like to come up on to the stage and help me?"

Immediately a forest of eager hands shot up. The Prince caught sight of the Brownies.

"That tall girl there," he called, pointing to Lesley, "and the little dark-haired one at the end. Will you come up quickly, please?"

"But Barbara didn't put her hand up!" whispered Lesley indignantly to Brown Owl, who sat behind them.

"Never mind! Go on, up you go, both of you!" Brown Owl whispered back.

"Right!" said the Prince. "Let's hear you two sing it through on your own, and then we'll ask everyone else to join in."

Lesley looked proudly out towards the audience where her friends were sitting. She took a deep breath and began to sing. Then a terrible thing happened! Her throat seemed to tighten up, and her usually strong voice became a tiny squeak. She felt like bursting into tears! The Prince laid a comforting hand on Lesley's shoulder. "Don't worry – stagefright!" he murmured.

Suddenly they heard a sweet, clear voice take up the tune. It was Barbara! Lesley glanced sideways at the small girl, who still looked timid and shy, but who was singing with her whole heart, and not a trace of the awkward stammer.

"That was very, very lovely," said the Prince at the end of the song. "We have performed this show many times for dozens of audiences, but I don't think we've ever had a singer like this young lady. Your Brownie friends must be proud of you!"

"We certainly are!" declared Lesley on the way home, when the entire bus was buzzing with excited chatter. "If it hadn't been for you beside me, I should have felt a right fool, Barbara! But why ever didn't you tell us you could sing like that?"

"Well," began the younger girl slowly, "my father ran away from home when he was young, to j-join an opera company. He had a fine voice, b-but he became ill and had to leave. He got a job in a factory, but he's always longed to return to the s-stage."

Brown Owl nodded understandingly.

"I've never let him know how much I-I love music," continued Barbara with growing confidence, "in c-case it brings back his own disappointment. But I do l-love to sing!"

"And you shall," promised Tawny eagerly. "I'll tell my sister I've found a promising new pupil that she simply *must* teach!"

"Barbara was brilliant!" said Paula. "But why didn't she stammer when she was singing, Tawny? It was magic!"

"Singing is one of the best cures for a stammer," Tawny told her. "And the more Barbara sings, the more confidence she will get when she speaks, so that she'll gradually lose her stammer altogether!"

And Barbara did.

AN EEE—SY PUZZLE

The 1st Easingborough Brownies are up in London for the weekend to explore as many sights as possible! Can you work out the names of the places they visited by filling in the missing letters — we've given you a few E's to make it EEEsier!

– – – – – E TUSSAUD'S
– – – E – BRIDGE
TRAFALGAR – – – – – E
THE – – – E – – E MUSEUM
WESTMINSTER – – – E –
PETTICOAT – – – E
– – – – – E ARCH

SHOWTIME

Our Brownie Pack is visiting the County Show but we've arrived early – so early that the Pets Display is still waiting for the animals to arrive! Each animal's pen was labelled with the name of the country or region it originally came from, so Brown Owl asked us to guess what kind of animal would be in each pen. See if you know them all!

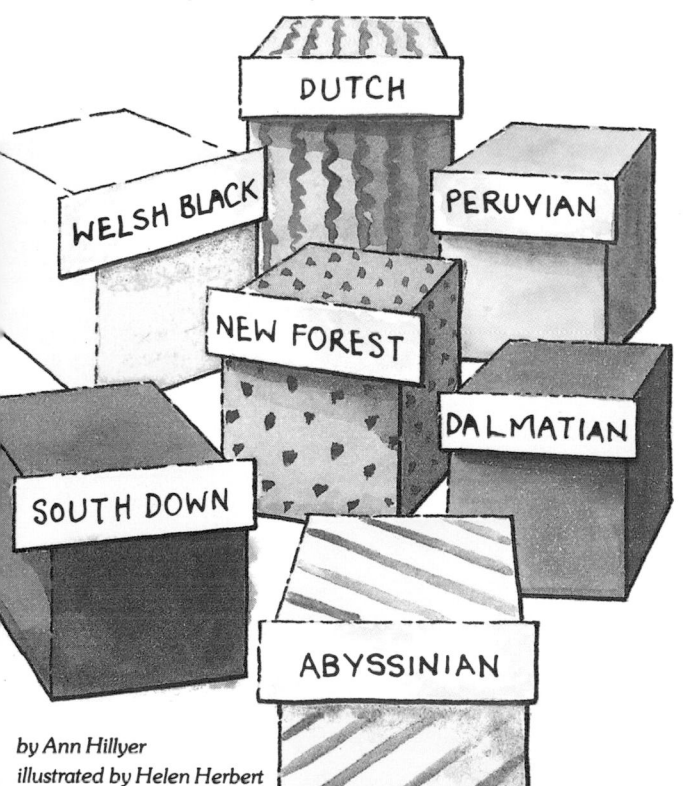

DUTCH
WELSH BLACK
PERUVIAN
NEW FOREST
DALMATIAN
SOUTH DOWN
ABYSSINIAN

by Ann Hillyer
illustrated by Helen Herbert

WHAT'S ON THE Menu?

Katie is trying hard to get her Cook Badge and is working out a breakfast menu for practice. Unfortunately her spelling isn't as good as her cooking! Can you help unscramble the items on Katie's menu so that the tester can read it?

lammadera
flonersack
stoat
preartigfu
canob
guessasa
rufit iceju
relace
laffsew
tracsions

The animals of
WAR

by Brenda Apsley
illustrated by Bob Hersey

You have probably heard about the George Cross and the Victoria Cross, medals awarded to people for bravery in wartime. But have you heard of the Dickin Medal? It too was awarded for bravery shown in wartime – but to animals.

Mrs Maria Dickin, the founder of the People's Dispensary for Sick Animals, realised that animals were playing an important part in the Second World War, often with great bravery. In recognition of this she set up the Dickin Medal, awarded to any animal displaying great gallantry and devotion to duty. It became known as 'the animals' Victoria Cross'.

The bronze medal has the PDSA initials at the top, the words 'For Gallantry' in the centre and 'we also serve' below. In all, 53 medals were awarded, 18 to dogs, 3 to horses, 31 to pigeons – and one to a cat!

Here are a few of their amazing stories . .

Many deeds of courage, duty and endurance were carried out by dogs during the war. **Judy** *was a pointer who was adopted as a mascot by the Royal Navy, serving on several gunboats before being torpedoed and captured by opposing soldiers. She spent two years as a prisoner of war in awful conditions. The guards tried to shoot her many times, but she always escaped their bullets, and helped to keep*

her fellow prisoners cheerful. She even saved lives by distracting the guards when they began beating prisoners, risking her own life in the process. She was released, along with the other prisoners, in 1945.

Jet *served with the Civil Defence workers in London. It was his job to sniff out people who were trapped under collapsed buildings during the air raids.*

Pigeons played a very important role during the Second World War, carrying messages and saving many lives. When a flying boat had to ditch near the Hebrides in Scotland one morning in 1943, bad weather and a very thick mist held up the rescue. But that afternoon a pigeon called **White Dove**, released by the crew when the plane came down, reached her home loft carrying details of their position. The search was started again and the men were rescued. White Dove had flown sixty miles over very rough seas and through thick mist to deliver her message. Without her the crew might have died.

Along with many other dogs like **Irma**, **Rip** and **Thorn**, Jet worked in very dangerous conditions amidst thick smoke and burning buildings. Ignoring falling debris and intense heat, he followed any scent that might lead to a buried survivor and saved many lives.

Rob served with the Special Air Service. He made over 20 parachute jumps, took part in the landings during the campaign in North Africa, and later served in Italy with a Special Air Unit. He acted as patrol dog and guard to small groups of men on dangerous missions in enemy areas. His keen senses saved many men from capture and allowed many missions to be completed successfully.

Many cats served as mascots with the Royal Navy, some for many years on the same ship. Their main job was to control the numbers of mice and rats, but they also acted as companions to the crew. **Simon** served on HMS Amethyst where, though wounded by shell blast, he kept at his job of catching rats, showing no fear in the awful conditions around him as the ship came under enemy fire.

Horses no longer served with the cavalry during the Second World War, but they played their part still, serving with the Mounted Branch of the Metropolitan Police in London. They endured anti-aircraft fire, bombs, fires and the noise and confusion of collapsing buildings, remaining on duty with their riders and helping to control traffic and rescue services. In April 1941, fire bombs fell close to the stables where police horse **Regal** was kept. Regal was alone, yet stood calmly, even when the stable caught fire, until help arrived and he was led to safety. Normally a horse would be driven wild with terror by fire. Three years later a bomb exploded nearby, and this time Regal was injured by flying fragments and covered by debris when the stable roof collapsed. But once again he remained calm and refused to panic.

Tea, please!

written by Brenda Apsley
illustrated by Nicola Heindl

Once upon a time in China, about 4,500 years ago, the emperor Shen Nung sat beside a fire, boiling some water to drink. Some leaves from a nearby shrub, caught by the wind, dropped into his water pot. The boiling water turned a pale gold colour and smelled good, so Shen Nung tasted it. Since that accidental 'brew', tea is now drunk all over the world . . .

Tea reached Britain in the 1660s, when Catherine de Braganza brought some as part of her dowry when she married King Charles II. The King liked the drink and it became popular at the royal court, soon taking the place of ale at the breakfast table!

When tea was first imported into this country it was heavily taxed – in the 1700s a pound of tea would have cost more than £60 in today's money. But in 1784 the tax was lowered and the habit of tea drinking spread.

In the eighteenth century fashionable ladies had started to offer tea to their guests. It was still expensive, and kept under lock and key in special boxes called caddies. The caddy was kept locked all the time and only the mistress of the house had a key.

Tea was served with great ceremony. Servants brought in a large tea tray complete with expensive china teacups and saucers, teapot and stand, sugar bowl and milk jug – and a slop basin for the discarded tea and leaves. The mistress of the house brewed the tea herself, and no well-brought-up young Englishwoman was a social success unless she could brew a good cup of tea.

Thomas Twining opened Tom's Coffee House in Devereux Court, London, in 1706. There were 2,000 coffee shops in London at that time, so as a gimmick to attract customers Thomas started selling a new drink – tea. His notices announced a stock of 'all sorts of fine teas, coffee, chocolate, coca-nuts, sago and snuff'.

Tea became a popular drink all over the world, and a part of the British way of life. We drink more than any other country – just under 200 *million* cups a day. That's about four cups each every day – about 1,500 per year!

In the seventeenth century a Dutch doctor told his patients that tea was good for them. He recommended that they drink 100 cups a day!

How to brew a perfect cup of tea

1
Fill a kettle with cold water fresh from the tap and bring it to the boil.

2
As the water comes to the boil, pour a little into an empty teapot to warm it. Pour away the water when the pot is warm.

3
Put some tea into the warmed pot — use one teaspoon for each cup and 'one for the pot'. If you are using teabags, use two for every three cups of tea.

4
Take the teapot to the boiling kettle. As soon as the water boils, pour it over the tea in the pot, put on the lid and allow the tea to brew — one minute for teabags and about three minutes for loose tea.

How to serve a perfect cup of tea

1
Set out teacups and saucers (china if possible).

2
Using a strainer to catch any stray leaves, pour the tea into cups.

3
Serve the tea on its own, or with a little milk and sugar, or a thin slice of lemon.

You can choose whether you like milk poured into the cup *before* the tea or *after*!

Thanks to Twinings for information and loan of transparency.

A special tea tray

To celebrate a special occasion like a birthday or anniversary, or just to say thank you, serve tea on a tray for someone special. Cover a tray with a pretty tray cloth, add a single flower in a tiny vase, and set the tray with a teapot, sugar bowl, milk jug and a pretty china teacup and saucer. Careful presentation makes all the difference, and tea served like this will taste much more special than in a mug at the kitchen table!

This giant teapot, probably the largest in the world, holds some 60 litres of tea – that's more than 300 cups. Chinese scenes showing growing, picking and shipping tea are painted around the teapot, which is 75cm high. It was probably made for the Great Exhibition in 1851, where it is said that Queen Victoria and Prince Albert drank tea from it. You can see it, plus lots of other tea-related exhibits, at the Twinings Tea Museum, 216 The Strand, London.

Tea is a refreshing hot drink, but it doesn't have to be drunk in the usual way, with milk and sugar. Try this spicy tea recipe...

Ginger up

1
Make a pot of fresh tea, allow to stand for a couple of minutes then measure out 300ml.

2
Mix with 300ml of apple juice and heat in a pan, but do not boil.

3
Put a teaspoonful of ginger in a heatproof tumbler or mug for each person.

4
Add the tea mixture, stir and serve. Add brown sugar to taste.

Tea makes a very refreshing cold drink, too, especially in summer. Here are two iced teas to try.

Spiced lemon tea

1
Cut a thick slice of fresh lemon and stick the sharp ends of five whole cloves into the skin.

2
Make a pot of tea. Earl Grey, a scented tea, is ideal for this if you have any.

3
Put the lemon slice into the teapot with the tea and leave to brew for three minutes. Remove the lemon.

4
Pour one tablespoon of fresh lemon juice into a heatproof tumbler and top up with tea.

5
Sweeten to taste with sugar or honey and serve with a cinnamon stick in each tumbler.

Apple tea

1
Make a pot of flowery Ceylon tea, strain it and chill in the fridge.

2
When it is cold, mix 300ml with 300ml apple juice. Pour over ice cubes in tall glasses.

3
Add a little sweetened lemon juice to taste. This is a real thirst quencher!

Tea eats

Tea can be used in cooking, and goes very well with fruits, as these recipes show!

Tea fruit salad

For four people you will need:
200g dried mixed fruits (whole apricots, prunes and apple slices are good)
600ml tea
strips of orange and lemon peel

1

Brew the tea, let it cool, then chill in the fridge.

2

Put the dried fruits into a bowl with the strips of orange and lemon peel and pour the cold tea over the mixture.

3

Leave the fruit to soak overnight in the fridge.

4

Next day, put the mixture into a pan, bring to the boil and simmer for ten minutes. The fruit should be just tender and the juices starting to thicken into a syrup.

5

Remove the orange and lemon peel and serve the fruit with a little of the syrup. Add cream if you like it, or plain yogurt.

Tea fruit loaf

200g packet mixed dried fruit
100g demerara sugar
150ml hot tea
1 tablespoon orange or lemon marmalade
1 egg
200g self-raising flour

1

Put the dried fruit and sugar into a bowl, pour over the hot, fresh tea, stir well and leave overnight.

2

Next day, preheat the oven to gas mark 4/350°F/180°C.

3

Beat the egg and add it to the fruit with the marmalade and flour. Mix well with a wooden spoon.

4

Grease a small loaf tin and pour in the mixture.

5

Bake for about 55 minutes until firm and golden or until a knife pushed into the loaf comes out clean. Serve on its own or spread with butter or honey.

All the way to Scotland

written by Deborah Manley
illustrated by Helen Herbert

Brown Owl's aunt has a farm in Scotland and in one of her fields there's a very special barn, with bunk beds and a real kitchen especially for Brownies. And this year we went there for Pack Holiday. It's a long way to Scotland from where we live, which is in London, so we had to spend a whole day on the coach.

We all took packed lunches with us to eat on the way. I shared mine with Hasina because her mum makes interesting spicy things that I like and my mum had made me egg and lettuce sandwiches which Hasina likes. We shared my chocolate bar too. But we ate that long before Brown Owl said that it was time for lunch.

We had to start very early in the morning. Dad took me and Jeannie, who's in my Six, to the hall where we have our Brownie meetings. That's where the coach collected us.

Brown Owl had given us a list of things to bring and said that we mustn't take too much else because we'd have to carry our own bags when we got to our destination. My bag was very bulgy and quite heavy, but I carried it all the way to the hall. I rather hoped though that our Pack Holiday home wouldn't be so far.

I thought Dad would never finish his breakfast and we'd be late for the coach. But it was all right and we were there long before some of the others.

Hasina was the last of our Six to arrive, but Alice had got there first and kept seats for us all at the back of the coach. So Hasina and I and Jeannie and Maria were all on the long back seat and Alice and Sharon had the next seat just in front of us.

When it was time to go we all kneeled up on the long back seat and waved goodbye to our families. And they all waved back until the coach turned the corner and they were out of sight. Then we were really on our way to Scotland. Maria looked rather sad as if she might want to cry. Sharon cheered her up by telling about how her little brother had eaten her chocolate bar for breakfast and got it all over his shirt and how cross her mum had been. Sharon always has a funny story to tell us.

We left London behind quite soon and we were right out in the country. It was a lovely sunny morning and we all looked out of the window and pointed out things to each other. The fields and trees looked so green and fresh after the city streets. Of course we've got a park near where we live, but it's not the same as being in the proper country.

We were on the motorway now. It goes on for miles and miles and it's not as interesting as proper country roads are. Soon we began to get bored.

"Are we nearly there yet?" asked Alice when we hadn't even reached Birmingham.

"Look," Hasina explained, taking out a pencil and a pad of paper. "This motorway, the M1, goes north and joins the motorway called the M6. The M6 goes around Birmingham and goes north like this all the way to Scotland right up here."

Alice looked at the map and sighed. "It's a long way, isn't it?"

It did seem a very long way.

"I know," I said, "let's play a game."

"In the coach?" asked Maria.

"Yes, listen. It's called Going to Scotland. At least that's what we'll call it today. I start by saying, 'I'm going to Scotland and in my bag I've packed,' and I say something beginning with A like '. . . an anorak.' Then you say the same, Maria, and add another thing beginning with the next letter of the alphabet."

"I'm going to Scotland and in my bag I've packed an anorak and a . . . a . . . bottle. Is that right?"

"Yes."

"Now it's my turn," said Hasina and she packed a cardigan.

Jeannie packed a duster, but Sharon had to make us laugh and after her elephant we packed some very odd things. We'd passed Birmingham and Stafford by the time we got to Z and our bags were full of all sorts of things that weren't on Brown Owl's list. We had the anorak, bottle, cardigan, duster and Sharon's elephant and then there was a fox, goose, horse, ice-cream, jack-in-the-box, knight in armour, lamb, mouse, netball, orange, peanut, queen, rabbit, sausage, table tennis table, unicorn, vase, whale, xylophone, yacht and, to finish with, a zebra.

"You'll never be able to carry all that!" said Brown Owl who had come to tell us we'd be stopping soon to go to the toilets. "And when we get back on the coach," she said, "it'll be time for lunch. Be sure you pick up every scrap of paper when you've finished."

I'd just finished my last bite of apple and popped the core into the plastic bag in which Maria had collected all our rubbish, when Jeannie suggested another game.

"It's called Pot of Gold," she said. "Someone starts by saying, 'If I found a pot of gold I'd

buy,' and then describes something. The others have to guess what it is. The one who guesses finds the next pot of gold."

"Let me start," said Sharon. "I've got a good one."

"Go on then," said Jeannie.

"If I found a pot of gold I'd buy something with checks and pleats."

We were all quiet for a bit while we thought about that.

Then Alice said, "Would it be made of wool?"

"Yes."

"You'd buy a Scottish kilt, wouldn't you?" said Alice.

"Oh, you've guessed!" said Sharon. "I should have chosen something more difficult."

"It's your turn now, Alice," said Jeannie.

Alice thought for a time and then she said, "If I found a pot of gold I'd buy something that's young and cuddly."

"Lots of things are young and cuddly," said Jeannie. "Can't you give us more of a clue?"

"Is it alive?" asked Maria.

"Yes."

"Does it bark and wag its tail?" I asked.

"Yes, you've guessed," said Alice.

"It's a puppy, isn't it?" I knew that Alice wanted a puppy. I tried to think of something really difficult. "If I found a pot of gold," I said, "I'd buy something that's very tall with a tall thing on top."

That kept them guessing for a long time.

"Is it a tower?" Jeannie suggested.

"No."

"Some sort of tree?" asked Maria.

"No."

"Is it alive?" Hasina asked.

"Yes, part of it anyway."

"Is the alive part a giraffe?" asked Sharon.

"Yes, but you've got to get the other part too."

They went on guessing for ages until Jeannie at last said, "Is it a giraffe in a top hat?"

And she was right.

After that our purchases with the pot of gold got more and more difficult. They included a holiday in Italy (that was Maria), a helicopter (that was Jeannie), a ride on Concorde to New York for Hasina and a golden tiara with a huge ruby for Sharon, who guessed about Concorde so she got another turn.

By that time Brown Owl came to tell us that we were now near the Lake District. She'd asked the driver to turn off the motorway so we could see some of the lovely country.

We stopped near Lake Windermere for a while. Brown Owl got us to play some games that made us run around and stretch our legs. Then she bought us each an ice-cream.

When we'd finished every last drip we clambered back onto the coach. For a time, while the coach went along the shore of Lake Windermere and then drove back to the motorway, we all looked out of the window.

Then Sharon said, "I've remembered a really funny game. We should really sit in a sort of circle to play, but Alice and I can kneel up and look over the back of the seat."

When they were ready, Sharon said, "Now I say, 'Mother Magee is coming to stay.' Then the next person, that's you, Hasina, says, 'What's she like?' And I say something like, 'She has her hand on her head,' and I put my hand on my head like this, and keep it there. Then Hasina says the same to you, Jeannie, then puts her hand on *her* head. It goes on like that round the circle until we've all got one hand on our head. Then Hasina starts next and says what Mother Magee is like and does that, but she keeps her hand on her head as well.

"You add all the ways of Mother Magee and keep the old ones too. But," said Sharon, "anyone who laughs – or even smiles – during the game is out."

We started slowly but, once we got going and really understood the game, we got faster. Mother Magee, and all of us, had one hand on her head, one eye shut, her tongue sticking out and was holding one ear when Sharon herself burst out laughing and, of course, all the rest of us joined in.

"It's not fair being here," giggled Sharon. "We see all of you along the back seat at once and you can only see the two of us properly."

Katie and Joss came to see what all the laughter was about and then they wanted to play too. This time they knelt on the seats opposite Sharon and Alice and we made two teams so the first team that laughed was the loser.

That didn't take long. Mother Magee only held her nose, patted her head and winked before Joss and Katie collapsed into giggles and our team won.

Then Brown Owl suggested that we might all have a singsong for the last bit of the journey. We sang *London Bridge is falling*

down and *One man went to mow a meadow* and then we started *There's a hole in my bucket.*

"There's a hole in my bucket, dear Liza, dear Liza,
There's a hole in my bucket, dear Liza, a hole.

Then mend it, dear Henry, dear Henry, dear Henry,
Then mend it, dear Henry, dear Henry, mend it.

With what shall I mend it, dear Liza, dear Liza,
With what shall I mend it, dear Liza, with what?

With straw, dear Henry, dear Henry, dear Henry,
With straw, dear Henry, dear Henry, with straw.

The straw is too long, dear Liza, dear Liza,
The straw is too long, dear Liza, too long.

Then cut it, dear Henry, dear Henry, dear Henry,
Then cut it, dear Henry, dear Henry, cut it.

With what shall I cut it?" we sang and the song went on:
With a knife;
The knife's too blunt;
Then sharpen it;
With what shall I sharpen it?
With a stone;
But the stone is too dry;
Then wet it;
With what shall I wet it?
With water;
In what shall I get it?
In a bucket;
But there's a hole in my bucket, dear Liza, dear Liza,
There's a hole in my bucket, dear Liza, a hole.

And it was just then that the bus slowed down and turned through a gate and there was Brown Owl's Aunt Jessie waiting to greet us.

"It didn't seem a very long way to Scotland after all, did it?" said Alice as we jumped down from the coach.

"I've got some more Mother Magees for the journey home," said Sharon and waved one hand in the air.

The Duck

Behold the duck.
It does not cluck.
A cluck it lacks.
It quacks.
It is especially fond
of a puddle or a pond.
When it dines or sups,
It bottoms ups.

Ogden Nash

From 'I wouldn't have missed it' by Ogden Nash, reprinted by permission of André Deutsch Limited.

illustrated by Jill Gibbon

29

WWF/Mike Corley

World Conservation and YOU

written by Liz Chidley

Dodo, dinosaur, duck – which is the odd one out? Duck! Why? Did someone throw something? No, a duck is the odd one out because you could go out tomorrow and see one. To see a dodo or a dinosaur you would need a time machine, because dodos and dinosaurs are both extinct. Horrible word, isn't it? – it means gone for good.

Although they have extinction in common, they became extinct in very different ways. The dinosaurs became extinct because the world altered and they could not cope with the changes. We could call this natural extinction. On the other hand, the dodos became extinct because sailors killed them and ate them for food – we could call this unnatural extinction. Extinction is a perfectly normal part of the world's natural history and in fact it plays an important part in keeping the world healthy. However, the sort of unnatural extinction that the dodo suffered from can cause all sorts of problems. Let me try to explain why.

Every animal and plant is designed to live in a certain way in a particular part of the world. Just look at pictures of different animals and plants and you will see how their colour and shape, for example, help them to live comfortably in a particular part of the world. A living thing's colour and shape are affected very much by the type of weather and surroundings it lives in. But weather and surroundings change only very slowly and stay the same for a long time. For example, the North Pole was cold and ice-covered when you were born and it will probably still be cold and ice-covered when your children's children's children are born. So you might think that animals and plants that are adapted to live there, such as the polar bear, with his thick white coat, should have a long and happy life ahead of them!

However, the world is constantly changing and the animals and plants that live on it are also adding their own little bits of change to it. Now this sort of change is a very slow process – you don't wake up one morning and find that your semi-detached in Croydon or Newcastle is under fifty metres of water, or is covered in forest, or surrounded by snow and ice that never goes away, even in the summer! But if you had been alive millions of years ago, your area could have been just like this. As time goes by, then, and weather and surroundings change, some animals can find that they have the wrong sort of coat or teeth or feet for living in those surroundings. If that happens, the species die out – they become extinct.

Now comes the complicated bit – changes that make the world inhospitable for some animals and plants make it ideal for others. So, as some species die out, others take their places. Therefore at any time in the world's history there are animals and plants that have been around for a long time and are doing well, some that are slowly dying out and others that are just beginning to do well. This happens so slowly that the world seems to be almost unchanging, and unless you were a scientist looking at it very carefully you would not even know it was happening.

When more and more humans came along, though, some of the changes began to happen much more quickly. The more people there are, the more food, houses and clothing they need. Nowadays, people want faster cars and bigger aeroplanes, clothes they can wash easily, food which is fast and easy to cook and lots of other things which our great-great-grandparents would never have dreamed of. All the materials which are needed for the things people want have to come from somewhere in the world and this is causing much bigger changes. We need to build factories for things to be made and houses to live in, so there is much less countryside. There are also many changes caused by pollution, when the waste from the factories and houses is dumped into the seas, rivers and lakes.

All these changes are affecting our world much more quickly and widely than ever before. Whenever somebody chops down a forest for example, they are not just killing the trees, but also all the animals who used to live in the trees and the plants which used to live in their shade. Whenever a factory is built, the animals and plants which used to live in the area before have to move on or be dug up and killed. Imagine this happening all over the world and it is clear to see how easy it is for many kinds of animals and plants to become extinct.

There are so many different kinds of animals and plants living on the earth that even the cleverest scientists don't know them all – so it is likely that many species have become extinct that we don't know about. We don't know what they do, whether they are important or even what they look like!

All this change is happening so quickly that the natural replacement of dying plants and animals with new ones cannot happen properly. This is wrong, because the health of the world which supports everyone is controlled by the living things and the natural processes which people are busily interfering with and upsetting. The World Wildlife Fund thinks that human beings should take better care of our world. If you agree, why not ask your Guider if the Pack can work for the Conservation Badge?

Liz Chidley is Education Officer of the World Wildlife Fund (UK).

WWF/Mike Corley

WWF/Mike Corley

WWF/Olwyn Sandbrook

WWF/Dave Currey

Animals
to make
Pompon panda

Pandas are rare, elusive mammals. They are solitary animals and spend about half their day eating huge quantities of bamboo shoots.

You will need:
thin card
a pair of compasses
scissors
a ruler
scraps of white knitting wool
and black felt
a large-eyed tapestry needle
glue

illustrated by Kim Collins

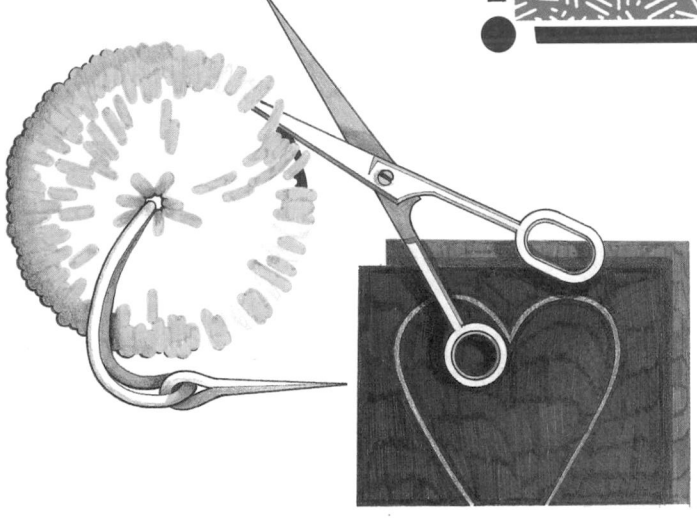

1. Cut out two card discs 8cm in diameter with centre holes measuring 3cm in diameter, and two 6cm discs with 2cm holes in the centre.

2. Thread the needle with a long double thread of wool and wind it round the two large card discs until the centre holes are full. Whenever the wool in the needle becomes too short, cut it and start again with another piece.

3. When the centre holes are full, slip the point of a pair of scissors through the wool and between the two discs. Wind a length of wool round several times between the discs and tie securely.

4. Cut the card discs and ease them off the pompon. Roll the pompon between your hands to form a ball.

5. Repeat this procedure using the smaller pair of card discs.

6. Trim any uneven ends of wool off the pompons and tie the small pompon on top of the larger one.

7. Stick a piece of black felt over a square of card and cut out an elongated heart shape for the panda's feet. Glue this to the underside of the larger pompon.

8. Cut out arms, ears, a nose and eyes for the panda from scraps of black felt and stick them in position.

Felt mouse

You will need:

brown and pink felt
scissors
string
glue
2 small black beads
1 large black bead
a needle and thread

House mice can be found almost anywhere people live and will eat almost anything we eat. In large numbers they are very destructive and spoil more food than they eat. These small furry animals have very good hearing and a keen sense of smell.

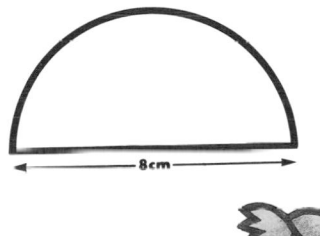

8cm

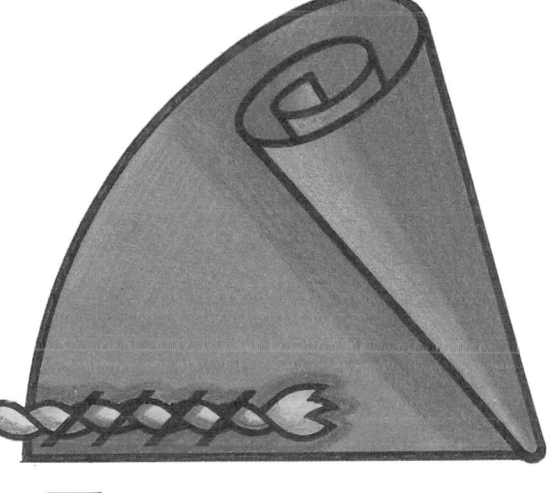

1 Cut a piece of brown felt into a semi-circle whose base is 8cm long. Sew a short length of string to the curved edge of the semi-circle to represent the mouse's tail, then roll the felt into a cone shape and glue it along one edge.

'Pompon Panda' by Gloria Wittke and 'Felt Mouse' first appeared in Art & Craft and were subsequently published in 'Animals to Make' by Scholastic Publications Limited in conjunction with the World Wildlife Fund – UK. Every effort has been made to trace contributors and if any right has been omitted The Brownie Annual offers its apologies.

2 Cut two small semi-circles of pink felt for the mouse's ears. Fold them in half and stitch them in position on the mouse's body.

3 Use two small black beads for the mouse's eyes and a larger one to represent the nose, stitching the eyes in position beneath the ears and the nose at the tip of the cone.

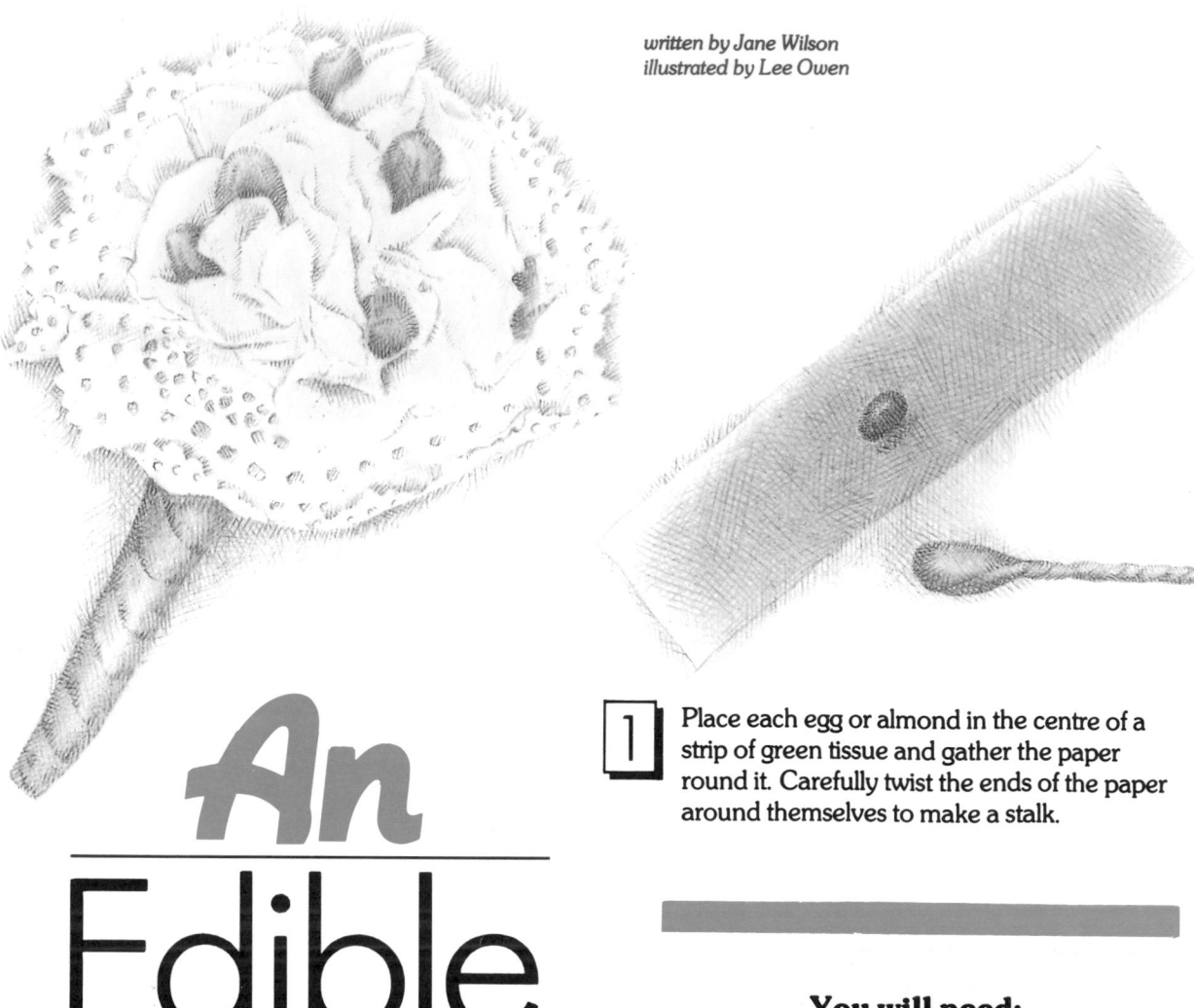

written by Jane Wilson
illustrated by Lee Owen

An Edible Posy

Here's a lovely present to make for Mum or an auntie for Mothering Sunday or Easter. Not only does it look pretty, but she'll be able to eat it too!

1 │ Place each egg or almond in the centre of a strip of green tissue and gather the paper round it. Carefully twist the ends of the paper around themselves to make a stalk.

You will need:

12 mini chocolate eggs or sugared almonds

12 strips of green tissue paper 7cm x 35cm

24 squares of yellow or pink tissue paper 6cm x 6cm

Scissors

Sticky tape

A paper doily 16cm across

A strip of green tissue paper 4cm x 45cm

Glue

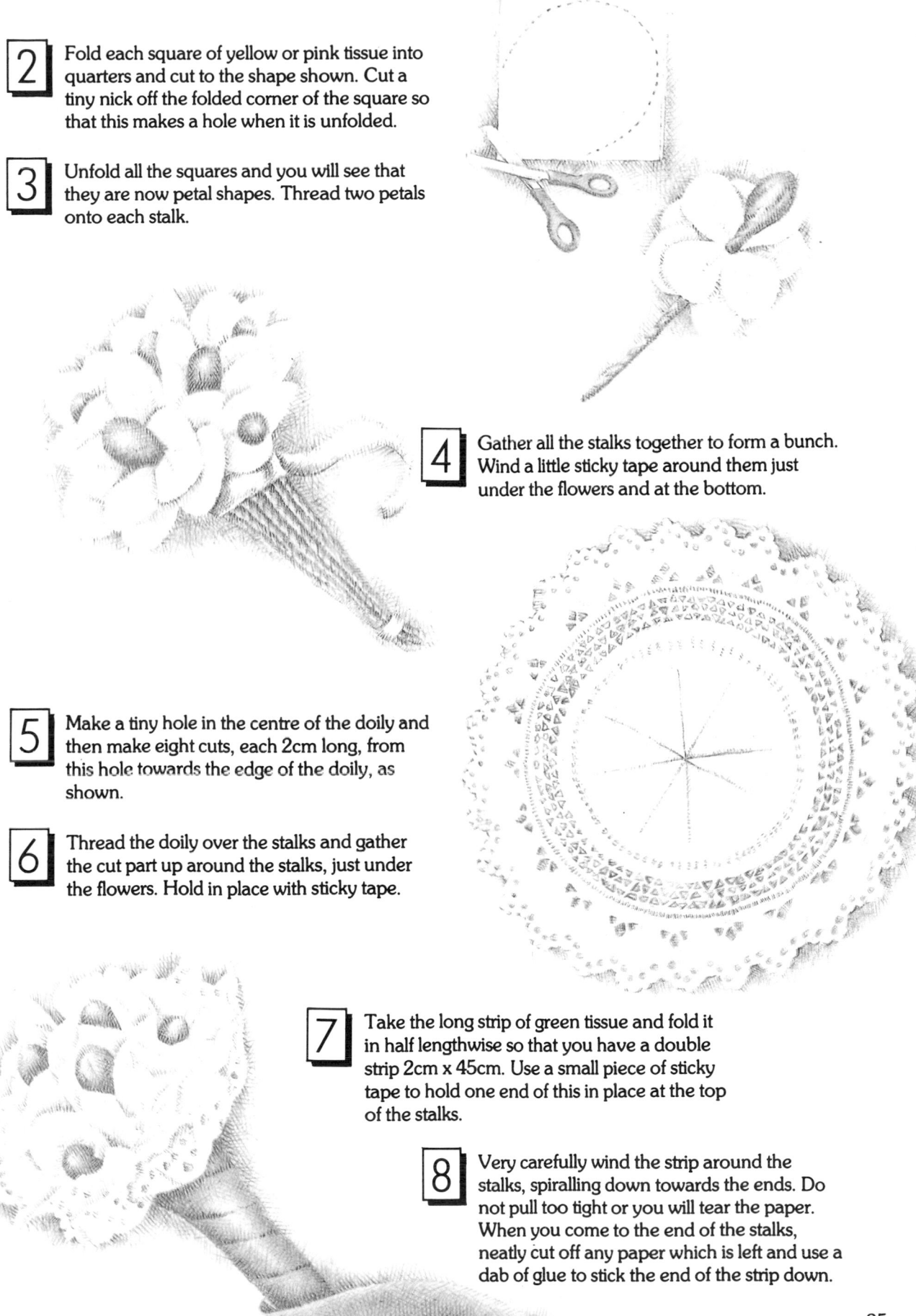

2 Fold each square of yellow or pink tissue into quarters and cut to the shape shown. Cut a tiny nick off the folded corner of the square so that this makes a hole when it is unfolded.

3 Unfold all the squares and you will see that they are now petal shapes. Thread two petals onto each stalk.

4 Gather all the stalks together to form a bunch. Wind a little sticky tape around them just under the flowers and at the bottom.

5 Make a tiny hole in the centre of the doily and then make eight cuts, each 2cm long, from this hole towards the edge of the doily, as shown.

6 Thread the doily over the stalks and gather the cut part up around the stalks, just under the flowers. Hold in place with sticky tape.

7 Take the long strip of green tissue and fold it in half lengthwise so that you have a double strip 2cm x 45cm. Use a small piece of sticky tape to hold one end of this in place at the top of the stalks.

8 Very carefully wind the strip around the stalks, spiralling down towards the ends. Do not pull too tight or you will tear the paper. When you come to the end of the stalks, neatly cut off any paper which is left and use a dab of glue to stick the end of the strip down.

35

Dance quiz

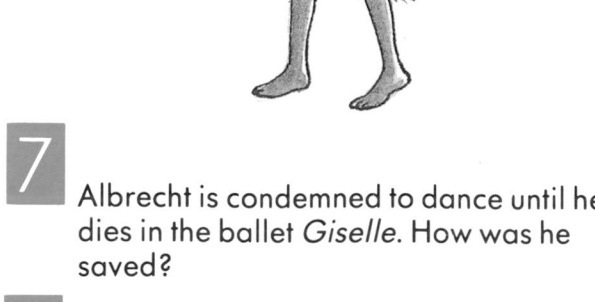

a.

b.

c.

written by Julia and Florence Nellthorp
illustrated by Helen Herbert

1 Which country do the dancers in these pictures come from?

2 What musical instrument would you expect to accompany them?

3 What was Coppelia in the ballet of the same name?

4 In which famous ballet do Siegfried and Odette throw themselves into the lake to escape an evil magician?

5 Which ballet is based on the Arabian Nights tales and is set in a harem?

6 Which fairy dances with the Prince in *The Nutcracker* ballet?

7 Albrecht is condemned to dance until he dies in the ballet *Giselle*. How was he saved?

8 For which types of dancing do you wear
a) a tutu?
b) metal toe-capped shoes?
c) bells and ribbons around the legs?

9 Unscramble the following to find four different types of dance
a) SOCID
b) MIBLO
c) ROMOLABL
d) DEARBACNIGKN

10 Which dance is the odd one out?
Tango, Waltz, Cha-cha, Rumba

(**Answers** on page 60.)

GIRL GUIDES

A Brownie's own garden

written by Gill Pawley
illustrated by Jane Winton

Each year, hundreds and hundreds of people get lots of pleasure from gardening. Have you ever thought about growing things? Many Brownies will already have a small garden of their own, but here are a few tips for those of you who want to start a new hobby.

You do not need to live in a house with a large garden to be able to grow things. Plants will grow happily in plant pots or troughs, on a window ledge indoors, on a balcony or in a corner of a patio, as well as in the ground.

One important thing to remember when you start gardening is that you must look after your plants all year round. Most of your work will be done in autumn and spring but you must keep an eye on things during the harsh winter months as well. Your garden will not be pleased with you if you only water it every six months!

We will give you some ideas in this feature, but you are bound to need some help as well. Everyone needs help when they first start as there is so much to learn about gardening. An adult who enjoys gardening is bound to be interested in helping you out – and this could be one of your parents, a grandparent, teacher or even Brown Owl!

How do you start?

Firstly, find out what kind of garden you can have. Mum or Dad will probably help. They will be able to let you have a piece of ground if there is room or show you where to put things if you are to be an indoor gardener.

Secondly, you will need to think about your soil. Soil in an outdoor garden should be as fine as possible. What you don't want is very hard ground where plants will find it difficult to get moisture and grow. The soil should be turned over until it is fine enough to run through your fingers when you pick some up. If it is a long time since anything grew in the soil or a large bush or tree has recently been dug up, the ground may not have all the things in it which are necessary for plants to grow. There are lots of different ways of putting goodness back into your soil, but you will need the help of an adult. Ask for advice before you start.

Compost is best if you are growing things in plant pots or a trough. Again, ask an adult for help. Compost can be expensive if you have lots of things to grow so you may need to shop around.

What are you going to grow?

If you are going to have a flower garden, a good way to start is with bulbs which flower in the spring. You plant the bulbs about September/October time and then you have to wait until the following February or March before you see any flowers. But there is nothing nicer than seeing lots of spring flowers after a hard winter. Bulbs which are easy to grow are daffodils, tulips, crocuses and snowdrops.

You do not need an outdoor garden to think about planting bulbs. Hyacinths are very popular for growing inside and can be grown in soil or water. A room which has a bowl of hyacinths in it always smells nice. Daffodils can also be grown indoors, as well as crocuses.

Bulbs are on sale in early autumn in garden centres, flower shops, large department stores

- Be patient. Getting the soil right is a very important part of gardening.
- If you are using clay plant pots, put some small stones in the bottom to help the water drain away.

and supermarkets. Remember when you plant them to go deep enough into the soil. About ten to fifteen centimetres for larger bulbs like daffodils and tulips and five to ten centimetres for smaller bulbs should be about right. If you don't put the bulbs deep enough, they could come to the surface when it is still frosty and be killed by the cold.

Other ways to start off your flower garden are from seed and from cuttings. Packets of seeds are quite cheap to buy and if most of the seeds grow, you will have plenty of plants – maybe too many, so you can share some with other people and they could do the same for you. Follow the instructions on the packet carefully – some seeds need to be grown in a greenhouse although many will grow happily on a sunny window ledge.

If you know anyone with a garden, you can ask for cuttings from plants they have. An adult should take the cutting for you and will probably give you growing tips as well.

How about growing plants from pips? Pip plants are grown indoors and are very easy. Orange and lemon pips are a good start. The pips should be dry and not cracked or broken. Fill a medium sized plant pot with compost and press three or four pips into it. Water well. Put a small plastic bag over the pot and secure with an elastic band – the bag is taken off when the pips begin to shoot. It will be a few weeks before you see any signs of life but once through

your plants will grow quickly. You will not get real lemons or oranges but you will have a lovely plant that has a slight perfume. Try grapefruit pips as well.

When it comes to vegetable gardening, you can grow a lot from seed. Mustard and cress are very easy to grow indoors, but other things like cucumbers are a bit harder. Many garden centres sell tomato and potato plants ready to go into the ground or plant pots. Keep your eyes open for advertisements especially in late spring.

Many Brownies will want to grow herbs. Herbs flower as well as having a nice smell. The best thing though is that you can use them in cooking and in making sweet smelling presents, like lavender sachets to put in a wardrobe. Nowadays, herbs are sold at supermarkets, flower shops and garden centres.

How do you look after your garden?

We have already said that a garden needs to be looked after all year round, but just what do you have to do to make sure your garden does not wither and die?

First, and very important, is watering. You should water your garden regularly – in summer this may need to be every day because hot weather dries the soil out quickly. You will soon get to know which plants need watering more than others. During winter, your garden will not need very much water but you will need to keep an eye on things.

Second, you should always look out for weeds. Weeds can even come through in plant pots! When you first start gardening, you may wonder which are the plants and which are the weeds. Ask your gardening adviser to point out the weeds for you. You do not want to allow the weeds a chance to grow and take the goodness out of the soil for your plants. A weed-free garden also looks much nicer!

Once you have done all the hard work to get the soil right when you start your garden, you won't want to let it become hard and unworkable again. So you should turn the soil over regularly

to keep it fine. You can use a hoe or a small hand fork to do this. Even the soil in plant pots needs to be gently turned over every now and then – a hand fork is fine for this.

Finally, you will want to keep an eye on the plants themselves. It is always a good idea to take any dead flowers or leaves off the plants because they are not doing any good. If you grow vegetables, there will be a very exciting time of year when you will be able to pick or dig up what you have grown. Remember that you should not pick vegetables too early as they will not have finished growing – either the seed packet or the shop where the plants came from

Tips to remember

- **In an outdoor garden, remember to put low plants at the front with taller ones at the back.**
- **When gardening indoors, always put saucers under your plant pots to catch any drips when you are watering.**

will give you instructions. Just think how proud you will be when you can give your mum a bunch of carrots, say, to cook for tea.

Herbs need harvesting at certain times of year to make sure they grow well the following year. Again, you should get instructions when you buy the plants.

Tips to remember

- **When you plant seeds outside, it is a good idea to put a tag in the ground to remind you where you planted them.**
- **If you are using plastic plant pots, you must remember to make sure that the plant does not outgrow the pot and become 'potbound'. If there are roots growing through the holes in the bottom of the pot, that is a sign that the plant needs to be transferred to a bigger pot.**

What tools will you need?

There are a few tools that you will find helpful when gardening. One is a small garden fork for weeding and putting plants in and the other is a long handled hoe which can be used for turning the soil over. Both these will cost lots of money to buy, so if your family does not

already have these or similar things, it is a good idea to borrow them. Brown Owl or your teacher may be able to help.

Look after your tools. Always clean them after use and replace any protective covers.

You will also need something for watering your garden – you do not need to have a watering can as a milk bottle or jug will do.

Tips to remember

- **If your soil is fine, you can use a plastic spade (like you find at the seaside) for turning the ground over.**
- **An old eating fork can be used to turn the soil in plant pots.**

What do you do next?

As we said earlier, you will need help when starting off – and, as many adults enjoy gardening, you should not have much trouble finding someone to give you advice. Every gardener makes mistakes when starting off so do not worry if you do not get everything right at first. You must be patient. Sometimes you will plant something and then have to wait a whole year before it flowers. But it will be worthwhile when you can go out and pick some flowers or someone compliments you on your bowl of hyacinths. You may also want to keep a garden diary. A good way of doing this is by taking photographs or drawing what is in your garden at different times of year.

Of course, some Brownies may not be able to have their own garden. If this is your case, perhaps you can help someone else or your school or Brownie Pack may have its own garden you could work on.

So, the next step is to find out more about gardening. You may find these books helpful – 'Garden Flowers' (Ladybird nature series), 'Discovering flowering plants' (Wayland Publishing) and 'Flowers' (Methuen Discoverers series). Try your local library for copies of these and other books.

Then you can think about where your garden will be and what you will grow there.

Whatever you do, good luck and good gardening!

Be a Discoverer!

written and photographed by Susan Tyte

Excited Brownie voices coming up the path told me that the 12th Kingswood Pack had arrived! They had come to spend the day working on the Discoverer Badge in Badminton Woods, near Bristol. I was to be their tester, so I had arrived early to plan trails for them to follow.

After pulling on their wellingtons and gathering up clipboards, the Brownies were off on the trails. Some of the instructions were easy to follow, some were more difficult. Everyone found a gate with bars, but the pine tree between the horse chestnut tree and the beech was harder to spot. The Brownies pulled out identification books to check – yes, they were right.

Soon they reached the end of the trail, where the parent helpers were waiting to explain what to do next. The Brownies had to observe seven living animals and seven living plants and be able to name them and discover something of interest about each of them. The Brownies went into the woods to look for their plants and animals. Whenever they found anything interesting they drew it or took photographs. They used identification books to learn more about the animals and plants they saw.

When they had finished this, I checked that everyone knew the Country Code. It's just common sense, really – do you know it?

Country Code

**Enjoy the countryside and respect
its life and work.**

•

Guard against all risk of fire.

•

Fasten all gates.

•

Keep your dogs under close control.

•

Keep to public paths across farmland.

•

**Use gates and stiles to cross fences,
hedges and walls.**

•

**Leave livestock, crops and
machinery alone.**

•

Take your litter home.

•

Help to keep all water clean.

•

Protect wildlife, plants and trees.

•

Take special care on country roads.

•

Make no unnecessary noise.

Why don't you ask your Guider if the Pack can work for the Discoverer Badge? Here's what you have to do:

1 Observe seven living animals and seven living plants. Be able to name and discover something of interest about each of them.

2 Following directions you have been given, take your tester to a spot unknown to you which will be not more than 300 metres away. To do this you may have to use a compass, follow signs on the ground, or look for growing trees or bushes or for landmarks. You may have to do any or more than one of these things.

3 Show during the test that you know the Country Code.

The Brownies ended the day by making 'Brownie Houses' and you can find out how they did that on the next page. As we went home, eighteen Brownies looked forward to getting their badges at the next Brownie meeting.

The Brownie Annual would like to thank the Duke of Beaufort and the Badminton Estate for their help in preparing this article.

Natural ideas

written by Susan Tyte
illustrated by Linda Costello

Keep the out-of-doors near you all year round with these nature crafts.

Bright impressions

Here's a way to keep summer colours with you even in winter.

several pieces of thick paper – blotting paper or sugar paper is best if you can get it
some heavy books
fresh petals from the garden – you must *never* pick or damage wild flowers or plants in the country.

1. Cut the paper into squares about 10cm x 10cm.
2. Look in your garden and collect a few petals – white daisies, golden buttercups, yellow dandelions. Ask your parents before you pick anything!
3. Place the petals and flowerheads carefully between the pieces of paper, as flat as you can.
4. Put the paper on a flat surface and pile the books on top of it. Choose a place where the books will not be disturbed for a few weeks.
5. Leave the pile untouched for about four weeks – this is a real test of your patience!
6. When the time is up, take the books away and gently slip the petals out of the paper. Put them in a bag or a box so that they can't blow away.

Brownie homes

Are you a Pixie? Or an Elf? Whichever Six you belong to, build your Brownie emblem a home.

You will need:

a plastic tray
small stones
some soil
bits of moss, twigs, leaves, grasses and so on (but remember – don't pick wild flowers!).

1. Cover the base of the tray with stones or soil.
2. Build a little house using the stones and some twigs, then cover the outside with moss.
3. Make a garden around the house from petals, moss, grasses and other natural bits and pieces. If you have one, you could include a mirror as a garden pool.

4. Finish off by making a model of your emblem from coloured pipe cleaners. See which Six can make the most interesting home for their emblem!

When you go on an outing with your Pack into the country or a park, take a look around you at all the lovely trees there are. Look at the different leaf shapes and colours, especially in autumn. If you find a leaf you would like to keep, you can turn it into a brooch.

Petal marks

This is a good way to display your pressed flowers and petals.

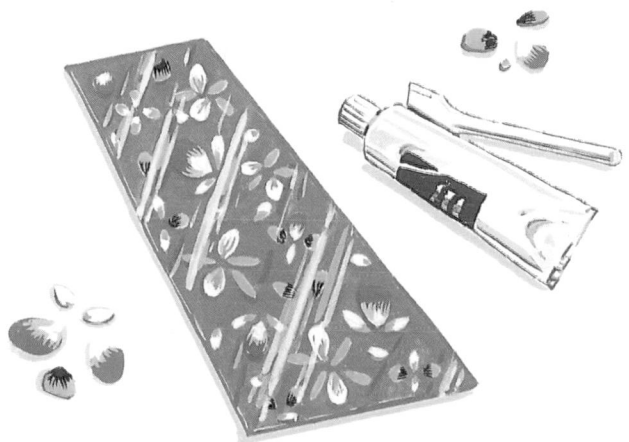

a piece of stiff paper or card
a tube of glue and a spreader
an old plastic carton lid
your pressed petals
scissors
clear sticky-backed plastic

1. Cut an oblong about 16cm long and 6cm wide from your card or stiff paper.
2. Arrange your petals in a pattern on the oblong.
3. Squeeze a blob of glue onto the lid and dip the tip of the spreader into it.
4. Lift up the first petal, put a tiny bit of glue onto the back of it and stick the petal back in the pattern.
5. Continue until you have stuck down all the petals. Don't sneeze!
6. When the glue has dried, cover your bookmark with the clear plastic.

Gold leaf

You will need:

your leaf
gold spray paint
newspaper
a piece of thin card, slightly bigger than your leaf
a piece of clear sticky-backed plastic about the same size as the card
a safety pin
sticky tape
scissors

(Gold paint is quite expensive, so you could ask your Guider if the whole Pack could make brooches and take the cost out of Brownie funds. Or if you don't have any paint, you can still make the brooch using a brightly-coloured leaf instead.)

1. Put the leaf onto the newspaper and spray it gold, following the instructions on the can. (It may be best to do this out-of-doors.) If you don't have paint then leave this part out – your finished brooch will look just as good!

2. When it has dried, place your leaf on the card.
3. Cut a piece of the clear plastic large enough to completely cover your leaf.
4. Peel off the backing and carefully cover the leaf and the card with the sticky plastic. This will protect the leaf and make it shine.
5. Now cut around the leaf, taking care not to cut into it.
6. Tape the safety pin to the card, leaving the pin free to fasten.

Now you have a new piece of jewellery for yourself or a friend!

Heidi meets Grandfather

from *Heidi* by Johanna Spyri
abridged by Brenda Apsley
illustrated by Jill Gibbon

From the village of Mayenfeld a footpath winds up through green and shady meadows to the foot of the mountains. The way is steep and leads to the summits above. On a clear sunny morning in June two figures climbed the narrow mountain path, one a tall girl called Dete, the other a younger girl called Heidi.

They came to the hamlet of Dorfli, halfway up the mountain. Here they met with greetings, for Dete was now in her old home. "Where are you off to with the child?" asked one. "I suppose it is the child your sister left?"

"Yes," answered Dete. "I am taking her up to her grandfather, where she must stay."

"The child cannot live with him," said the other. "He will have nothing to do with anybody. The mere sight of him, with his bushy grey eyebrows and beard, is alarming."

"Well, he is her grandfather and must look after the child," said Dete.

After a long climb they reached the top of the mountain. Here stood Grandfather's hut.

He was sitting on a seat, his pipe in his mouth and his hands on his knees, looking out. Heidi was at the top first. She went straight up to the old man, put out her hand and said, "Good evening, Grandfather."

"What is this?" he asked gruffly as he gave the child an abrupt shake of the hand, and gazed at her from under his shaggy eyebrows. Heidi stared steadily back at him.

"Good day," said Dete. "I have brought Heidi. I have done my duty by her for four years, and now it is your turn."

"What am I to do with her?" asked Grandfather.

"That is your affair," said Dete. "I had to put up with her when she was left on my hands. Now I have to look after my earnings, and you are the child's next of kin."

Grandfather rose from his seat and looked at her in a way that made her draw back, then he said, "Be off with you, and do not let me see your face again in a hurry." Dete did not wait to be told twice.

The old man went back to his bench, staring at the ground. Heidi stood and gazed at him, then said, "I want to see the house."

The old man opened the door and Heidi found herself in a good-sized room. In it were a table and chair and a cupboard. In one corner stood Grandfather's bed, and in another was the hearth with a large kettle hanging over it. Heidi looked around the room and asked, "Where am I to sleep, Grandfather?"

"Wherever you like," he answered.

Heidi was delighted and began to explore all the nooks and corners. Near Grandfather's bed she saw a short ladder against the wall. Up she climbed and found herself in the hay loft. There lay a large heap of sweet-smelling hay, and through a round window she could see right down the valley. "I shall sleep up here, Grandfather," she called. "It's lovely. But I shall want a sheet; you can't have a bed without a sheet."

"All right," said Grandfather. He went to the cupboard and drew out a long, coarse piece of material which was all he had for a sheet. He carried it up to the loft, where he found that Heidi had already made quite a nice bed, with extra hay at one end for a pillow. The two together spread the sheet over the bed.

"The bed looks lovely," said Heidi. "I wish it was night, so that I might get inside it at once."

"I think we might have something to eat first," said Grandfather. The kettle soon began to boil and the old man held a piece of cheese on a long fork over the fire, turning it round and round until it was toasted a nice golden yellow colour. He laid the toasted cheese on a layer of bread and filled a bowl with milk and told Heidi to eat. The cheese and bread tasted delicious.

The time passed happily until evening. "Now go up to bed," said Grandfather. "Sleep well."

"Goodnight, Grandfather," said Heidi, and climbed up to her bed, where she was soon lying as sweetly and as soundly asleep as any young princess on her couch of silk.

Bread and cheese

— a perfect combination

As Heidi found, bread and cheese make a delicious combination. Here are some simple bread and cheese recipes to try.

• Cheesy toasts •

Golden, melted cheese on toast, just as Heidi and Grandfather ate it. For each person you will need:
1 thick slice bread
a little butter
50g Cheddar cheese
¼ teaspoon mild made mustard
salt and pepper

1. Toast the bread on one side only.

2. Grate the cheese and mix with the mustard, salt and pepper.

3. Butter the untoasted side of the bread and spread the cheese mixture on top.

4. Grill until the cheese is melted and golden.
   (If you like, add thin slices of tomato on top of the cheese before grilling.)

• Fried cheese sandwich •

For each person you will need:
2 thick slices bread
2 slices processed cheese
1 slice cooked ham
a little butter and oil for frying

1. On one slice of bread, put a slice of cheese, a slice of ham, another slice of cheese and top with the other slice of bread.

2. Melt a little butter and oil in a frying pan.

3. When the oil is hot, fry the sandwich for about two minutes until it is golden brown. Turn it over and fry for another two minutes.

4. Remove from the heat and drain on kitchen roll.

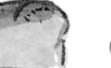

• Alpine eggs •

Heidi and Grandfather lived together in the Swiss Alps. Perhaps they ate this dish!
For two people you will need:
4 eggs
200g Cheddar cheese
15g butter
salt and pepper
1 small French loaf

1. Preheat the oven to gas mark 4/350°F /180°C.

2. Grease a small ovenproof dish.

3. Grate the cheese and put half into the dish.

4. Break the eggs into the dish, without breaking the yolks.

5. Season the eggs with salt and pepper. Pile the rest of the grated cheese on top.

6. Dot the butter over the cheese and bake in the oven for 15 minutes, until the eggs are set and the cheese bubbling.

7. Heat the French loaf in the oven for the last five minutes of the cooking time and serve in slices with the Alpine Eggs.

• Cheese and bread kebabs •

For each kebab you will need:
1 slice of bread about 2.5cm thick
50g Edam cheese
15g butter

1. Preheat the grill.

2. Cut the crusts off the bread and cut the bread into 2.5cm cubes.

3. Cut the cheese into 2.5cm cubes.

4. Melt the butter in a small pan and dip the bread into it. Make sure that each side of the bread is coated with melted butter.

5. Thread cubes of bread and cheese onto a kebab stick, first bread, then cheese, then bread again and so on.

6. Cook under the grill for about five minutes, turning, until the bread is golden and the cheese is starting to melt.

• Cheesy bacon nests •

For each person you will need:
1 large bread bap or bun
a little butter
1 rasher of streaky bacon
1 egg
1 slice processed cheese

1. Preheat the oven to gas mark 3/325°F/160°C.

2. Using a 5cm fluted pastry cutter, cut a circle in the middle of the bap, but don't cut right through – leave the base intact. This makes a bread 'nest'.

3. Butter the inside of the nest.

4. Grill or fry the bacon until crispy, then cut into small pieces. Put the bacon pieces into the nest.

5. Break the egg into the nest and bake on a baking sheet in the oven for about 20 minutes until the egg is set.

6. Put the slice of cheese on top and bake for another five minutes.

7. Put the bread 'lid' on the nest and serve.

Remember

* Always ask an adult before you start cooking.
* Tie hair back, wash hands and put on an apron before you begin.
* Clear away as you go and wash up afterwards!

Looking at Logos

by Charlotte Evans

Have you ever wondered what a logo is? Well, if you have, all will soon be revealed, and if not, then here's your chance to put that right.

You might say that a logo was 'short for' something – a quick and easy way to remind people of, say, a shop or a type of drink or a car or a pop group. It's a special symbol which many people use to make sure that something can be recognised very quickly by the general public. You can see examples of logos around the page.

The word 'logo' comes from a printing term 'logotype' which comes from the time when books and newspapers were printed using tiny metal letters made up into words. A logotype was a single piece of type which was made up of two or more letters. Nowadays a logo can include more than just letters, as you can see from the logos here. Most people who have logos make special rules about how they may be printed and what colours must be used and what shape the letters must be, so that wherever the logo appears it always looks the same. Sometimes a logo might even include a piece of music or a special song if it is being used in television or radio advertising.

Probably the simplest logo you could think of would be your own initials on something that belongs to you. It shows that the article is yours, so you can see why companies want to do the same thing. British Home Stores, for example, used to have their full name as a logo – which was very long and awkward! But now they have changed their 'image' and the inside of their shops and so they use a much more up-to-date logo. (Can you find it here?) The sloping multicoloured 'h' shows that the company is go-ahead and exciting, while the more traditional 'B' and 'S' stand for help to make customers think that the company is friendly

and reliable. The logo appears on everything – the store front, on clothes labels and hangers, carrier bags and delivery lorries. They even have a version in Arabic, which no doubt keeps their name even in the minds of the local camels! Most large shops do this – you should be able to find logos all over your home if you look carefully. I wonder if you know what C&A stands for (I'll tell you at the end of the article if you don't – but no cheating!).

What do you associate with the colour red – apart from Christmas and cherries? The Post Office, of course. They have their own particular shade of red (and yellow too) which adorns all their vans and post boxes. The Post Office even has its own specially drawn alphabet called Post Office Double Line (for obvious reasons!). The reason for this special alphabet is that it is an industry which relies on words to describe its services – no animal or picture could represent all it does.

Using colour is a very popular way of distinguishing your particular company especially if you have many rivals offering the same service. Banks, for example, use single colours – light blue for Barclays, green for Lloyds, orange for NatWest. To enhance this many use a symbol which does not necessarily have to be directly connected to the business. What, for instance, do horses and griffins have to do with looking after your money? Instead they

Lloyds
Bank

Royal Mail

GIRL GUIDES

communicate other qualities. The unbridled horse used by Lloyds depicts power and energy, an image which improves the rather staid atmosphere of banking.

Many companies choose logos which refer to their roots. The McDonald's chain of restaurants does this. Their symbol is not, as you might have thought, a golden 'M' but instead refers to the design of the very first McDonald's which opened in Des Plaines, Illinois, USA in 1955. Their logo, known as the Golden Arches, is based on the structure of the restaurant which was built using two large arches. When you looked at it from the side the two arches formed the Golden Arches of their logo. The colour was chosen simply because yellow is bright and highly visible from a distance, something which is very important in a crowded high street.

The National Trust's emblem also uses the idea of history but in a national sense. They had to find a logo that was anything but highly visible so that it did not look out of place when placed on mountainsides, in woods and meadows or on ancient buildings. The logo was originally designed in 1936. Six well-known artists and designers were asked to submit drawings incorporating either the English lion, the oak or the rose. Oak leaves were chosen because they were a less common heraldic symbol than a lion or a rose. The

National Trust for Scotland uses a thistle as its logo, carrying on the same theme of using traditional plants.

Older still than the National Trust's logo is the Times Clock Device which was first used in 1804. On the clock the time of 4.30 is shown, but this was not just picked out at random. Instead 4.30 a.m. indicates the agreed time when the printing of all London morning newspapers should have been completed. Also used in their logo are oak leaves and acorns to the left of the clock which suggest trustworthiness, and laurel leaves to the right which are a symbol for future glory in reward for present virtue, two qualities which are of vital importance to a national newspaper.

As you can see, a lot of thought goes into the making up of a logo. All organisations have very strict rules about how to make sure that their logo always appears just as it should be because, just by itself, it stands for the whole organisation. Isn't it surprising how much work goes on behind such a seemingly small thing?

Oh! before I forget C&A stands for Clemens and August Brenninkmeyer, the original founders of the company – what an interesting fact to stun your friends with!

The Brownie Annual would like to thank all those companies and people who have allowed us to reproduce their logos here.

Brownie mittens

To fit ages 7 – 8 years,
length variable.

You will need

25 grams tan double knitting yarn
oddments of dark brown,
skin-coloured and yellow yarn
scraps of red, blue and hair-coloured yarn

pattern by Angela Schofield
photograph by Dave Woolford

Using size 10 needles and tan yarn, cast on 36 stitches. Work 14 rows in k1 pl rib. Change to dark brown and knit 1 row, purl 1 row (this is the Brownie's belt). Change back to tan yarn and k18 stitches. Make 1 by picking up the loop before the next stitch and knitting into the back of it. This is called m1. Knit to end. Purl next row.

Continue in tan: k18, m1, k1, m1, k18. Purl next row. Continue to increase two stitches on each knit row, one each side of the thumb gusset, purling back until there are 49 stitches.

Next row, k31, turn, p13. Working on these central 13 stitches (for the thumb), work 10 rows in tan. Change to skin-coloured wool (for hand) and k2 together across row. P2 together across next row. Break off yarn leaving a length of about 25cm. Thread this through a sewing needle and pick up the remaining stitches. Fasten off the hand.

Return tan yarn to base of thumb on right side of work and pick up 2 stitches (same method as m1). Work to end of row (38 stitches).

With tan yarn, beginning with a purl row, work 6 rows in stocking stitch (1 row knit, 1 row purl). (You can knit more rows if you need them.) Break off tan and continue in skin colour for 6 rows (Brownie's face). Break off skin colour and use dark brown for hat. Next row: k1, k2 together, k14, k2 together, k1, k14, k2 together, k1 (beginning to decrease for hat point). Next row purl.

Continue to decrease 4 stitches on each knit row until 2 stitches remain. Purl these together and leave a thread about 30cm long. Thread the end through a sewing needle as for hand and sew hat seam.

Join rest of thumb, face and body by sewing neatly (overstitch) in yarn of correct colour. Turn to right side.

Using scraps of yarn, embroider eyes, mouth, buckle on belt, a Six emblem and two dark brown buttons. Work a crossover tie in yellow and a tiny French knot in silver parcel string for a Promise Badge! For hair, work embroidery in your own hair colour (plaits or bunches are easiest). Complete top of hat with a small brown pompon.

(For extra security join a length of brown ribbon or single crochet to each mitten and pass down sleeves!)

Win a rucsac!

You all know that Brownies have fun out-of-doors – enter our super competition and win a Brownie-sized rucsac for days out with the Pack!

Go anywhere with your Karrimor 'Diddy' daysac.

There are three Karrimor 'Diddy' daysacs to be won in this year's Brownie Annual competition by Brownies who like getting out and about. All you have to do is answer the following five questions and tell us what your favourite Brownie outdoor activity is and why on the coupon below.

1. **Where was Olave St Clair Soames born?**
2. **Which town did Heidi's grandfather live near?**
3. **Which animal eats bamboo shoots?**
4. **Why might you recognise part of the Australian flag?**
5. **What was the name of the man who discovered tea?**

You will find all the answers somewhere in the pages of this Annual!

Twenty runners-up will receive a copy of *Taking care of Carruthers* by James Marshall.

Name ....

Address ....

....

Pack ....

Date of birth ....

Answers:

1 ....

2 .... 3 ....

4 ....

5 ....

My favourite Brownie outdoor activity is ....

because ....

....

Why not send in the form on page 60 as well?

It's Winter. Carruthers Bear is feeling ill and miserable, and his medicines don't make him feel at all better. 'Perhaps I'm not long for this world,' he says morbidly. 'My stars,' says Emily, 'don't be ridiculous.' Something clearly has to be done, so Eugene Turtle begins to tell a story about three friends, Carruthers, Emily and Eugene, who one Summer's day take a trip downriver and have some extraordinary adventures – and soon even Carruthers is completely absorbed . . .

The Brownie Annual reserves the right to substitute similar prizes should those illustrated not be available for any reason.

The Brownie Annual would like to thank Karrimor International Limited and Fontana Young Lions, part of the Collins Publishing Group, for their kindness in donating the prizes for this year's competition.

Be a Brownie birdwatcher

written by Gill Pawley
illustrated by Mark Viney

Do you enjoy watching birds? Do you know the different birds that live in your area? Wouldn't it be a funny world if there were no birds at all – we wouldn't be able to listen to bird song or watch them swooping and whirling in flight – and the number of insects would soon get out of hand.

People go birdwatching for lots of different reasons; because of the songs the birds sing, the colour of their feathers or because of the way they fly or often just the challenge of finding different birds is enough. Dedicated birdwatchers travel hundreds of miles to get a glimpse of one bird. Very often, they can identify a rare one by its song or a flash of the bird in flight and they keep detailed records of all they see.

However, you do not need to travel great distances to see birds, for they live everywhere. Wherever you live you can be a Brownie birdwatcher – and that includes big cities. In fact, in the last few years more and more birds have got used to living in towns and cities, and so it isn't just very common birds like sparrows and pigeons which can be seen.

Becoming a birdwatcher

It really is easy to become a birdwatcher – it mainly depends on keeping your eyes open! Unless you want to develop birdwatching into a serious hobby you will not need much equipment – a notebook to write down details of the birds you see will be enough to start with.

A good idea is to get to know the birds living in your area. You will probably recognise two or three types of birds already. By getting hold of a book about birds, you will soon be able to identify others.

In towns and cities, you can look forward to seeing magpies, jays, bluetits and robins if you keep your eyes peeled. If you live in the countryside, you may already be used to seeing swallows, great tits, chaffinches and yellowhammers. A coastal area will have a different collection of birds – like plovers, curlews, redshanks or gulls.

Birds living in towns and cities are generally tamer than those in the countryside and by the coast. This is because the town and city birds are used to more people and traffic.

One of the key secrets to successful birdwatching is patience. Remember that no matter how tame they become, birds are still wild creatures and will be frightened away by sudden movement or noise. Some birds will feed at the same spot every day but others will be shy and you may have to wait for many hours before seeing the bird you want. But this is one of the excitements of watching birds – will the robin show up today? Or will the bluetit stay long enough for you to draw it?

Feed the birds

If birds know that food is regularly put out for them, they will quickly get into the habit of visiting a bird table, garden or a window ledge at the same time each day. This may become especially important during winter when food will be scarce and the birds are very hungry. You need not put food out between April and September when the birds should be able to find enough to eat. But do remember that in winter you may be the only source of food for birds in your area and they will become dependent on you. So, once you start to put food out, do try to carry on. Feeding birds is a good way of getting to know their habits without moving from your home.

Here are some ideas to get you going:

- Many birds, you may be surprised to know, like cheese! But it should be grated first before being put out.
- Blackbirds and thrushes like bruised and rotten apples. You can also put dried fruit out.
- Bluetits are well known for liking nuts. You can buy special bags from pet shops which the birds hang on to while pecking at the nuts.
- Everyone thinks that birds like bread, but dry, white bread can be difficult for them to eat, so soak the bread in water first.
- Your local birds will be very grateful for a dish of water at any time of year. Not only can they drink the water, but they can have a bath in it as well! Remember to change the water regularly.

The place you live will dictate what food you can supply. For example, if there is a bird table in your garden, that is obviously the best place to put any food. On the other hand, if you only have a balcony the ideal thing for you may be a bag of nuts to attract bluetits. You could also try putting a small amount of food on an outside window ledge each day.

Some things to remember

- Do tell your parents that you are going to feed the birds. They may wonder why the bread is not going as far as usual!
- Once birds know they can rely on you, you may get many visiting your feeding station – and they can cause a mess with droppings. Remember to clean the area regularly, as well as supplying fresh food and clearing away any old stuff.
- Cats are very fond of birds – but to eat, not to watch. If you have a cat, or there are some in the area you live, do try to make sure they can't get at the birds while they are eating. Squirrels, too, can cause problems. If you put nuts out, squirrels may rip at the bag or gnaw at the holder, causing damage. If this happens you will have to think up some clever plan to outwit the squirrels!
- If you live in a flat owned by the local council, you may find that you have to be careful not to encourage pigeons which are a pest in many cities. Ask your parents or Brown Owl for advice.

Date | Bird | where seen | Activity | Comments

·Puzzle out· Australia

written by Jane Wilson
illustrated by Jill Gibbon

Hello there!
My name's Peta and I'm a Brownie in Australia. We're called Brownie Guides here, just like you are, but as you can see our uniform is a bit different – probably because we have more warm weather than you do! Our Promise Badge is similar to yours, showing the Brownie man surrounded by a trefoil, but underneath is a boomerang with Australia written on it.

Here are some puzzles to help me tell you a bit about my country. Australia is a very big place, so big that the United Kingdom could be fitted into it more than thirty times! However, much of the land is uninhabitable and about a third of it is actually desert. Only 15 per cent of Australians live in rural areas, the rest of us live in towns.

The first inhabitants of Australia were the Aborigines, but in 1770 Captain James Cook arrived on the east coast and claimed it for Britain. He called the area where he landed New South Wales. The first European settlement was founded at Sydney Cove by people who we call the 'First Fleeters'. Many of them had committed crimes and been sent to Australia as a punishment. In later years people from many European countries and from Asia decided to seek out a new life in Australia. Australia no longer belongs to Britain, but is a member of the Commonwealth.

There are six states in modern Australia and each one is represented by a symbol on our Australian flag. To find out what that symbol is and what the flag looks like you'll have to colour in the picture below. You might recognize part of it!

B=blue R=red W=white

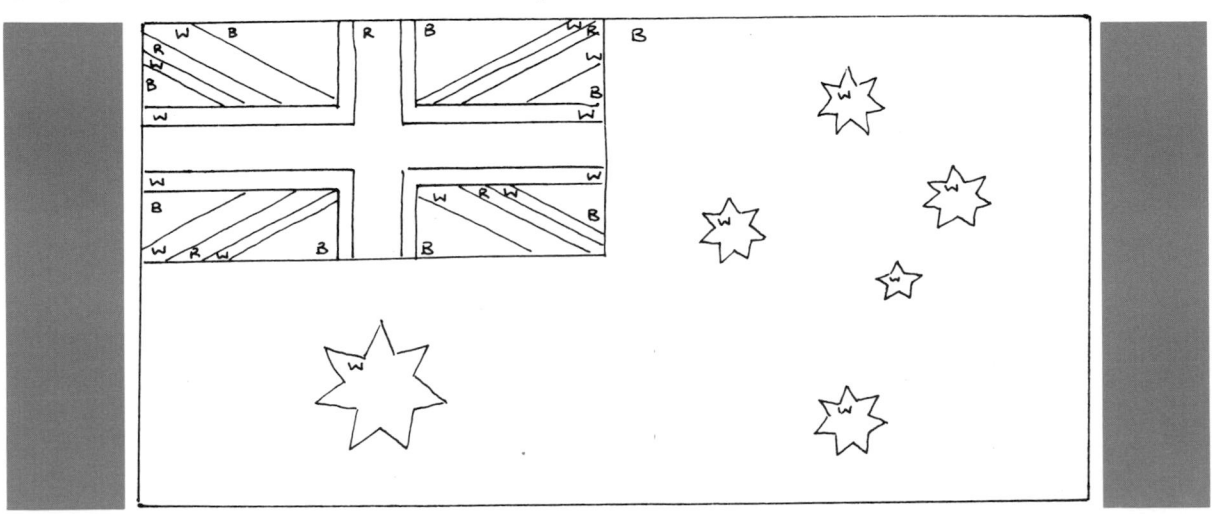

We have many plants and animals in Australia which are not found anywhere else in the world. One of the best known Australian plants is the eucalyptus or gum tree which koala bears love to eat. Perhaps you have sung the song 'Kookaburra sits in the old gum tree', well a kookaburra is an Australian bird. It is sometimes called the 'laughing jackass' because its noisy call sounds like laughter. Five Australian creatures, a kangaroo, a koala, a duck-billed platypus, an emu and a kookaburra are hiding in the picture above – can you help the Brownies to spot them?

Because the Australian people have their origins in so many different countries, we eat a wide variety of types of food, but steak and seafood are two things for which Australia is particularly famous. During our long summers we like to have lots of picnics and barbecues. In the Queensland area lots of tropical fruit is grown, including pineapples, bananas and peaches. Much of this fruit is put into cans in huge canning factories and is exported to other countries. You could look out for Australian peaches next time you help with the shopping.

One lovely Australian dessert is called Peach Melba as it is said to have been invented for a famous Australian opera singer called Dame Nellie Melba. All the ingredients you need to make this dish are hidden in the word square on the right – see if you can find all six.

(Answer on page 60.)

J	C	F	F	M	W	G	V	D	O	Q
A	K	O	V	A	R	S	T	U	N	H
N	E	T	S	E	C	T	B	A	R	T
V	G	Z	N	R	P	A	K	X	E	N
S	E	F	I	C	E	C	R	E	A	M
U	U	A	E	O	A	F	U	M	E	T
G	C	I	F	F	C	Y	I	A	R	D
A	V	O	T	L	H	L	T	D	Z	G
R	A	S	P	B	E	R	R	I	E	S
J	E	L	E	N	S	U	T	T	I	Y
A	N	G	N	O	N	B	A	P	P	L

Three Butterflies

Flat on my back
beneath the freckling sun,
three butterflies sail around me,
and very gently, one
settles on my burning face,
folding his dusty wings,
as if he liked the place;
and one hovers a little while
before he decides to land
with cool and delicate feet
upon the thumb of my right hand,
but soon changes his mind and does not stay
to keep me company, skimming soundlessly away
into the flowers and trees:
and one goes flitting around
my head at perfect ease,
and will not be my guest.

But how glad I am
that two of them made me
their resting place a minute or so,
believing I was a flower or a tree.

Leonard Clark

*From 'The Singing Time',
by Leonard Clark, reprinted
by permission of Hodder & Stoughton Ltd.*

Illustrated by Helen Herbert

Awake asleep

You will love this doll who is awake and dressed until you turn her over and then she is asleep in her nightie!

You will need:

50cm of 115cm wide flesh-coloured fabric
sewing cotton to match fabric
fabric scraps for clothing — some suitable for a nightdress and some for a daytime dress
100cm bias binding
3 small buttons (optional)
scraps of felt for eyes, mouth, etc; or coloured felt-tipped pens
kapok or scraps of material for stuffing
paper for pattern
scissors and other sewing equipment

written by Julia Nellthorp
illustrated by Caroline Bland

Enlarge and transfer the patterns of the doll and clothes (overleaf) onto the paper. Ask an adult to help you with this.

Trace the outline of the doll onto double-thickness flesh-coloured fabric and carefully cut out. (You will find it easier if you pin both thicknesses of fabric together.)

Trace the outlines of the dress and nightie onto single thicknesses of fabric. Cut carefully around the outlines.

Neaten the dress neckline with bias binding or lace if you have it.

Clip the bottom edge of the dress between points A and B.

Using an iron, press under a 1cm hem between points A and B (the edge you have already clipped will lie flat because of the clips).

7

Pin the dress in position over the doll body, right sides facing upwards. Stitch carefully along the hemline, using tiny running stitches.

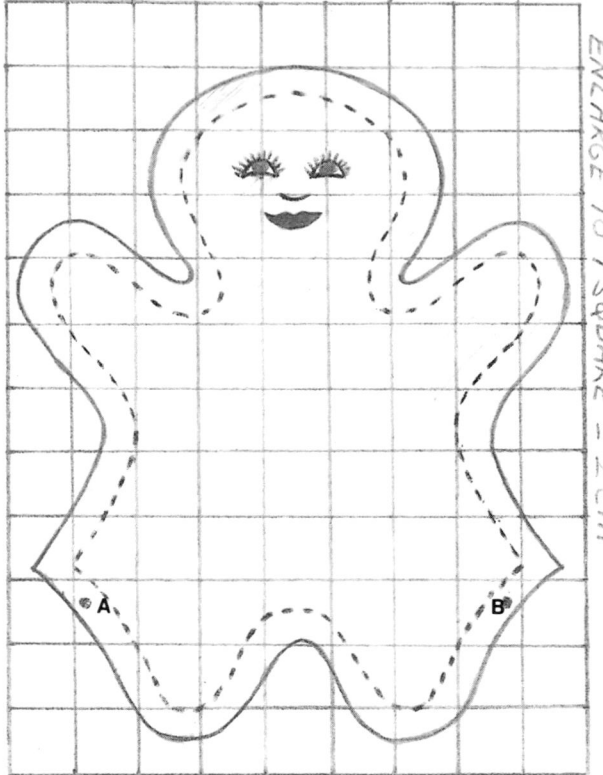

ENLARGE TO 1 SQUARE = 2 CM

8

Sew carefully up the sides and round the arms to join the dress to the body, turning the cuffs of the sleeves under neatly.

9

Decorate the front of the dress with buttons or lace if you like.

10

Bind the nightie neckline with bias binding. Clip, pin and sew to the other doll body shape as you did the dress.

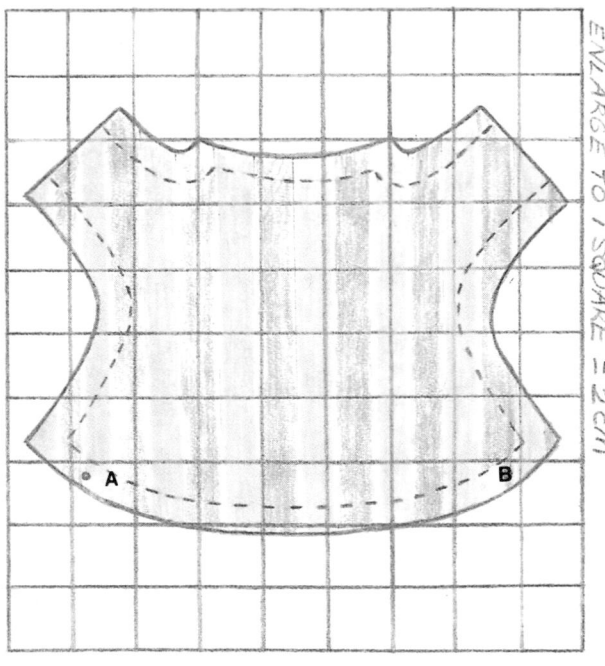

ENLARGE TO 1 SQUARE = 2 CM

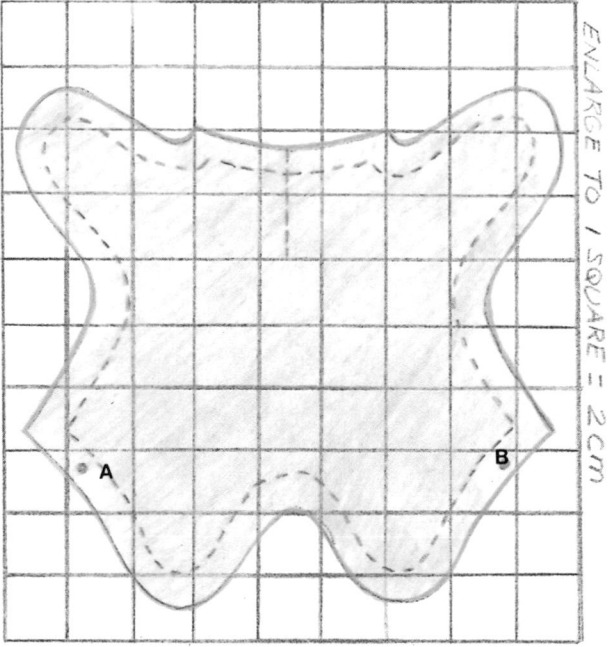

ENLARGE TO 1 SQUARE = 2 CM

Pin the doll front to the doll back with the right (dressed) sides facing one another. Carefully stitch around the outline, keeping 1cm away from the edge all the time, leaving an 8cm gap at the top of the doll's head. Trim the seams and clip so that there are no lumpy bits in the seam when you turn the doll the right way out.

Carefully turn the doll the right way out and stuff her with kapok or other soft fabric scraps. Stitch the 8cm opening up, using small, neat stitches.

Make eyes, noses and mouths for each 'face' of the doll from felt, or draw them on. Don't forget that the night-time doll should have her eyes closed!

Stitch some wool scraps on the doll's head for hair.

Answers

What's on the menu?
(page 19)
Marmalade
Cornflakes
Toast
Grapefruit
Bacon
Sausages
Fruit Juice
Cereal
Waffles
Croissant

Showtime (page 19)
Abyssinian cat
Dutch rabbit
New Forest pony
Dalmatian dog
Welsh Black cow
Peruvian Guinea Pig
South Down sheep

An EEE-sy puzzle (page 19)
Madame Tussaud's
Tower Bridge
Trafalgar Square
The Science Museum
Westminster Abbey
Petticoat Lane
Marble Arch

Dance Quiz (page 36)
1. (a) Spain
   (b) Scotland
   (c) Hawaii
2. (a) Castanets/guitar
   (b) Bagpipes
   (c) Steel guitar
3. A lifelike doll
4. Swan Lake
5. Scheherazade
6. The Sugar Plum Fairy (in the Kingdom of the Sweets)
7. Giselle danced too and sustained him until dawn when the Wilis' spirits had to go back to their graves.
8. (a) Ballet
   (b) Tap
   (c) Morris Dancing
9. (a) Disco
   (b) Limbo
   (c) Ballroom
   (d) Breakdancing
10. The waltz is the odd one out, because the rest are Latin American.

Puzzle out Australia word square (page 55)

J	C	F	F	M	W	G	V	D	O	Q
A	K	O	V	A	R	S	T	U	N	H
N	E	T	S	E	C	T	B	A	R	T
V	G	Z	N	R	P	A	K	X	E	N
S	E	F	I	C	E	C	R	E	A	M
U	U	A	E	O	A	F	U	M	E	T
G	C	I	F	F	C	Y	I	A	R	D
A	V	O	T	L	H	L	T	D	Z	G
R	A	S	P	B	E	R	R	I	E	S
J	E	L	E	N	S	U	T	T	I	Y
A	N	G	N	O	N	B	A	P	P	L

A message from the Editor

By the time you read this, I shall be beginning to prepare the *1991* Brownie Annual! This is because to produce a book like this can take such a long time that I have to start very early.

You can help me decide what to put into the 1991 Brownie Annual by filling in this form telling me what you liked most in this year's Annual and what you would like to read in a future one. Send it to: The Editor, The Brownie Annual, The Girl Guides Association, 17–19 Buckingham Palace Road, London SW1W 0PT.

I hope you enjoyed this year's Brownie Annual. Help me to make the 1991 Annual even better!

Name ....

Address ....

....

....

Pack ....

My favourite things in the 1989 Brownie Annual were:

1 ....

2 ....

3 ....

I would like to read in the Brownie Annual about:

....

....

....

The World Centres

Do you know you have four holiday houses around the world? Well, if you're a Brownie, you are part of the World Association of Girl Guides and Girl Scouts (WAGGGS) and *they* (that means *you*) have four special Guide houses – one in Switzerland, called 'Our Chalet', one in London, called 'Olave House', one in India, called 'Sangam' and one in Mexico, called 'Our Cabana'. They are friendly places where Guides and Girl Scouts from all over the world can meet one another and work and play together.

Olave House, the World Centre in London,

is not big enough for all the people who want to stay there, so Guides and Girl Scouts all over the world are helping to raise money for a new World Centre in London. This will be called the Olave Centre and will include a new Olave House and a headquarters building for WAGGGS.

You can help! Ask your Guider to find out about the Olave Centre and how you can raise money to help build it!

Even if you can't visit the World Centres in person just at the moment, you can still play . . .

The World Centres Game

HOW TO PLAY

Two, three or four people can play this game. You can either use buttons or tiddlywinks as counters or make your own 'flag' counters as shown below.

Each person chooses a country where there is a World Centre (India, Mexico, Switzerland

or the United Kingdom) and starts by putting her counter on the Promise Badge belonging to that country.

Throwing the dice, the players move in a clockwise direction around the board. (If you throw a six you get another turn.) Whenever a player lands on a square with a question on it, she cannot move on until she has answered the question correctly. The answers to all the questions are in the *Brownie Handbook* or the *Brownie Guide Badge Book*.

The object of the game is to get right around the board once and then up the centre 'spoke' to the World Badge in the middle. The first player to throw the right number to arrive on the badge wins.

Make your own flags!

India

Mexico

Switzerland

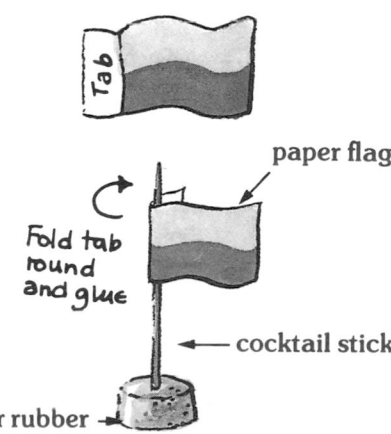

United Kingdom

Tab

Fold tab round and glue

paper flag

cocktail stick

cork or rubber

illustrated by Helen Herbert

Our Cabana, Mexico

What are the names of the Brownie Journeys?

How old do you have to be before you can join Brownies?

Why do we use three fingers when we salute?

Which Six emblem shows a little man with a broom?

Who started Scouts and Guides?

How much does a 999 call cost?

Our Chalet, Switzerland

What were Brownies called when they began in 1914?

Who was the World Chief Guide?